Inner Calm: Essential Meditations To Reduce Stress And Anxiety

Negoita Manuela

Published by Negoita Manuela, 2024.

While every precaution has been taken in the preparation of this book, the publisher assumes no responsibility for errors or omissions, or for damages resulting from the use of the information contained herein.

INNER CALM: ESSENTIAL MEDITATIONS TO REDUCE STRESS AND ANXIETY

First edition. March 30, 2024.

ISBN: 979-8223894971

Written by Negoita Manuela.

Table of Contents

Chapter 1: Introduction

- OVERVIEW OF THE BOOK and its purpose

Written by renowned leadership expert Dr. Emily Johnson, the book provides a deep dive into how digital technologies are reshaping the way organizations operate and how leaders can adapt and thrive in this new era. With a blend of practical advice, real-world case studies, and cutting-edge research, this book is essential reading for anyone looking to understand the intersection of leadership and technology.

Overview of the Book

In "Leadership in the Digital Age," Dr. Johnson begins by examining the fundamental shifts brought about by digital technologies, from the rise of artificial intelligence to the increasing interconnectedness of the global economy. She then delves into how these changes are reshaping traditional leadership models and pushing leaders to develop new skills and mindsets. With a focus on agility, adaptability, and innovation, the book outlines a roadmap for leaders to navigate the complexities of the digital age and drive their organizations forward.

Purpose of the Book

The primary purpose of "Leadership in the Digital Age" is to provide an accessible and actionable resource for leaders looking to thrive in the fast-changing world of technology. Dr. Johnson aims to demystify the digital landscape and empower leaders with the knowledge and tools they need to succeed. By offering practical strategies, real-world examples, and expert insights, the book equips leaders with the confidence and competence to lead effectively in today's digital-driven world.

Key Themes

Throughout the book, several key themes emerge that underscore the challenges and opportunities of leadership in the digital age. One of the central themes is the need for leaders to embrace change and uncertainty. In a world where technology is constantly evolving, leaders must be willing to adapt and experiment with new ideas and approaches. This requires a willingness to take risks, learn from failure, and continuously iterate to stay ahead of the curve.

Another key theme is the importance of fostering a culture of innovation within organizations. As digital technologies disrupt traditional business models, leaders must cultivate a culture that encourages creativity, experimentation, and collaboration. By creating an environment where employees feel empowered to take risks and explore new ideas, leaders can unleash the full potential of their teams and drive innovation throughout the organization.

Furthermore, the book emphasizes the critical role of ethical leadership in the digital age. With the increasing use of data and AI in decision-making, leaders must grapple with complex ethical considerations around privacy, transparency, and accountability. By upholding high ethical standards and promoting a culture of integrity, leaders can build trust with stakeholders and demonstrate their commitment to responsible leadership in a digital world. Through a blend of practical strategies, real-world examples, and expert insights, Dr. Johnson provides a comprehensive overview of the key challenges and opportunities facing leaders in today's fast-changing world. By embracing change, fostering innovation, and upholding ethical standards, leaders can position themselves to thrive in the digital age and drive their organizations to new heights of success.

- Importance of finding inner calm in today's fast-paced world

In today's fast-paced and hectic world, it is more important than ever to find inner calm in order to maintain mental, emotional, and physical well-being. The demands of modern life, including work, family, and social obligations, can often lead to high levels of stress and anxiety. This can have a detrimental impact on our overall health and happiness, making it essential to prioritize finding moments of peace and tranquility in our daily lives.

One of the key benefits of finding inner calm is the ability to manage stress more effectively. When we are constantly in a state of stress and anxiety, our bodies release cortisol, a hormone that can have negative effects on various systems in the body, including the immune system, digestive system, and cardiovascular system. By finding moments of calm and relaxation, we can help reduce the levels of stress hormones in our bodies and promote a sense of well-being.

In addition to managing stress, finding inner calm can also improve our mental clarity and focus. When we are constantly bombarded with distractions and information overload, it can be difficult to concentrate and make sound decisions. By taking time to quiet the mind and focus on the present moment, we can improve our ability to think clearly and make better choices in our daily lives.

Furthermore, finding inner calm can have a positive impact on our emotional well-being. When we are able to cultivate a sense of peace and tranquility within ourselves, we are better equipped to handle difficult emotions and situations with grace and resilience. This can lead to improved relationships with others and a greater sense of overall happiness and fulfillment.

There are many different practices and techniques that can help us find inner calm in our fast-paced world. Mindfulness meditation, for example, involves paying attention to the present moment in a non-judgmental way. This can help us cultivate a sense of inner peace and awareness that can carry over into our daily lives.

Yoga is another valuable tool for finding inner calm. The physical postures and breathing exercises practiced in yoga can help us release tension and stress from the body, while also calming the mind and promoting relaxation. Regular yoga practice can help us cultivate a sense of balance and serenity that can carry over into all aspects of our lives.

In addition to these practices, spending time in nature can also help us find inner calm. Whether it's going for a walk in the park, sitting by the ocean, or simply spending time in the garden, being in nature can help us connect with the world around us and cultivate a sense of peace and harmony within ourselves.

It is important to remember that finding inner calm is a process that takes time and effort. It may require us to make changes to our daily routines and habits, as well as to prioritize self-care and relaxation. However, the benefits of finding inner calm are well worth the effort, as they can lead to improved mental, emotional, and physical well-being in our fast-paced world. By prioritizing moments of peace and relaxation in our daily lives, we can better manage stress, improve mental clarity and focus, and cultivate a greater sense of emotional well-being. There are many practices and techniques that can help us find inner calm, such as mindfulness meditation, yoga, and spending time in nature. It is important to remember that finding inner calm is a process that takes time and effort, but the benefits are well worth it. By making self-care and relaxation a priority, we can cultivate a sense of peace and tranquility that can carry over into all aspects of our lives.

Chapter 2: Understanding Stress and Anxiety

- DIFFERENCE BETWEEN stress and anxiety

Stress and anxiety are two of the most common mental health challenges that individuals face in today's fast-paced and demanding world. While they are often used interchangeably, it is important to understand that stress and anxiety are distinct experiences with unique characteristics and effects on the body and mind.

Stress is a natural response to challenging or threatening situations, often referred to as the "fight or flight" response. When faced with a stressor, such as a tight deadline at work or a conflict in a relationship, the body releases hormones like cortisol and adrenaline to prepare for action. This can result in physical symptoms such as increased heart rate, muscle tension, and shallow breathing. While stress can be a motivator and help us perform better in certain situations, chronic stress can have detrimental effects on our physical and mental health.

On the other hand, anxiety is a more prolonged and intense feeling of unease, worry, or fear that can persist even in the absence of an immediate threat. Unlike stress, which is a reaction to a specific trigger, anxiety is often more generalized and can be triggered by a variety of situations or thoughts. Individuals with anxiety may experience symptoms such as racing thoughts, restlessness, difficulty concentrating, and panic attacks. Anxiety disorders, such as generalized anxiety disorder, social anxiety disorder, and panic disorder, are characterized by excessive and persistent worry that interferes with daily functioning.

One key difference between stress and anxiety is the nature of the threat or trigger that initiates the response. Stress is typically a response to a specific external event or circumstance, while anxiety often involves internal worries or fears that may not have a clear cause. For example, a student may experience stress before an exam, but someone with anxiety may feel overwhelmed by irrational fears of failure or judgment.

Another important distinction between stress and anxiety is the duration and intensity of the symptoms. While stress is usually temporary and can be resolved once the stressor is removed or managed, anxiety can persist over a longer period of time and may require professional intervention to address. Individuals with chronic stress may experience burnout or physical ailments like headaches or digestive issues, whereas those with anxiety may struggle with intrusive thoughts, avoidance behaviors, and difficulty coping with daily tasks.

It is also worth noting that stress can sometimes trigger or exacerbate anxiety symptoms, creating a cycle of heightened emotional distress and physical tension. For example, a person under chronic stress may develop anxiety symptoms as a result of the prolonged strain on their nervous system. In these cases, it is important to address both the underlying stressors and the anxiety symptoms to promote overall well-being and resilience. While stress is a natural response to challenging situations that can be beneficial in moderation, anxiety involves persistent worry and fear that may require professional support to manage effectively. By understanding the differences between stress and anxiety, we can better recognize and address our own emotional responses and take proactive steps to promote mental wellness.

- Common triggers for stress and anxiety

Stress and anxiety are common experiences that most individuals face at some point in their lives. In today's fast-paced and demanding world, it is not uncommon for people to feel overwhelmed and anxious due to various triggers. Understanding the common triggers for stress and anxiety can help individuals identify and manage these feelings more effectively.

One common trigger for stress and anxiety is work-related stress. Many individuals experience high levels of stress in their jobs due to long hours, tight deadlines, and a demanding workload. This can lead to feelings of overwhelm, burnout, and anxiety. Additionally, job insecurity, lack of control over one's work environment, and conflicts with coworkers or superiors can also contribute to stress and anxiety in the workplace.

Another common trigger for stress and anxiety is financial stress. Money problems, such as debt, unexpected expenses, and not being able to make ends meet, can cause significant stress and anxiety for individuals. The fear of not being able to provide for oneself or one's family can be a powerful stressor that can lead to anxiety and feelings of helplessness.

Relationship issues can also be a significant trigger for stress and anxiety. Conflicts with romantic partners, family members, or friends can create emotional turmoil and contribute to feelings of stress and anxiety. Lack of communication, misunderstandings, and unresolved conflicts can all take a toll on one's mental health and well-being.

Health issues, both physical and mental, can also be common triggers for stress and anxiety. Chronic illnesses, acute health crises, and mental health disorders can all cause significant distress and anxiety for individuals. The uncertainty of one's health, the fear of the unknown, and the challenges of managing a health condition can all contribute to feelings of stress and anxiety.

Life transitions, such as moving to a new city, starting a new job, or going through a divorce, can also trigger stress and anxiety. Change can be challenging and unsettling, and navigating unfamiliar territory can create feelings of uncertainty and insecurity. Coping with the unknown and adjusting to new circumstances can be stressful and anxiety-provoking for many individuals.

To summarize, societal and global issues, such as political turmoil, natural disasters, and the ongoing pandemic, can also be common triggers for stress and anxiety. The constant barrage of negative news and uncertainty about the future can create feelings of fear, helplessness, and anxiety in individuals. Coping with these external stressors can be challenging, but finding ways to manage stress and anxiety in the face of adversity is crucial for maintaining one's mental health and well-being. Understanding the common triggers for stress and anxiety, such as work-related stress, financial stress, relationship issues, health problems, life transitions, and societal pressures, can help individuals identify and address these issues more effectively. By recognizing the sources of stress and anxiety in one's life, individuals can develop coping strategies and seek support to manage these feelings and improve their overall well-being.

- How stress and anxiety impact our mental and physical health

Stress and anxiety are common experiences that affect individuals across the globe. While everyone experiences stress and anxiety to some extent, prolonged or chronic feelings of stress and anxiety can have detrimental effects on our mental and physical health. In order to better understand how stress and anxiety impact our overall well-being, it is important to recognize the ways in which these conditions manifest, the potential causes of stress and anxiety, and the strategies we can employ to manage and alleviate these feelings.

First and foremost, it is important to differentiate between stress and anxiety. While both are emotional responses to challenging or threatening situations, stress is typically a short-term reaction to a specific event, such as a deadline at work or an upcoming presentation. On the other hand, anxiety is a more generalized feeling of unease or fear that persists over a longer period of time and is often disproportionate to the actual threat. Despite their differences, both stress and anxiety can have profound effects on our mental and physical health.

One of the ways in which stress and anxiety impact our mental health is through cognitive changes. When we are stressed or anxious, our brains are flooded with cortisol, a stress hormone, which can impair our cognitive functioning. This can manifest as difficulty concentrating, memory problems, and impaired decision-making. In addition, chronic stress and anxiety can contribute to the development of mental health conditions such as depression and anxiety disorders. These conditions can further exacerbate feelings of stress and anxiety, creating a vicious cycle that is difficult to break.

Furthermore, stress and anxiety can also have a significant impact on our physical health. When we are stressed or anxious, our bodies enter into a state of heightened arousal known as the "fight or flight" response. This response is meant to help us deal with immediate threats, but when activated repeatedly or for prolonged periods of time, it can have negative consequences on our physical well-being. Chronic stress and anxiety have been linked to a variety of physical health problems, including cardiovascular disease, digestive disorders, and weakened immune function.

There are a number of potential causes of stress and anxiety, including environmental factors, genetic predisposition, and life experiences. For some individuals, stress and anxiety may be triggered by specific events or situations, such as a demanding job or a tumultuous relationship. For others, these feelings may be more pervasive and difficult to pinpoint. It is important to recognize that everyone experiences stress and anxiety differently, and what may be stressful for one person may not be stressful for another.

Fortunately, there are a variety of strategies that can help us manage and alleviate feelings of stress and anxiety. One of the most effective ways to combat stress and anxiety is through relaxation techniques such as deep breathing, meditation, and mindfulness practices. These techniques can help to calm the mind and body, reduce cortisol levels, and promote a sense of well-being. In addition, regular exercise, a healthy diet, and sufficient sleep are essential for managing stress and anxiety and promoting overall health. By understanding the ways in which stress and anxiety affect us, recognizing the potential causes of these conditions, and implementing effective strategies for managing and alleviating these feelings, we can work towards achieving a greater sense of well-being. By taking care of our mental and physical health and seeking support when needed, we can navigate the challenges of stress and anxiety with resilience and grace.

Chapter 3: Benefits of Meditation

- EXPLORING THE BENEFITS of meditation for reducing stress and anxiety

In recent years, there has been a growing body of research supporting the benefits of meditation for reducing stress and anxiety. Meditation is often touted as a powerful tool for promoting mental well-being and cultivating a sense of inner peace. This ancient practice has been used for centuries in various cultures and traditions to calm the mind and develop a deeper awareness of oneself. In today's fast-paced world, where stress and anxiety are all too common, meditation offers a natural and accessible way to unwind and find a sense of balance amidst the chaos.

One of the key benefits of meditation is its ability to quiet the mind and promote relaxation. By focusing on the present moment and letting go of distracting thoughts, meditation encourages a state of mindfulness that can help alleviate stress and anxiety. When we are constantly bombarded with external stimuli and racing thoughts, it can be difficult to find a sense of calm and clarity. Meditation provides a space for us to disconnect from the outside world and turn inward, creating a sense of peace and tranquility that can carry over into our daily lives.

Moreover, research has shown that regular meditation practice can lead to physical changes in the brain that are associated with reduced stress and anxiety. Studies have found that meditation can increase the activity in areas of the brain that are responsible for regulating emotions, such as the prefrontal cortex. This can help individuals better cope with challenging situations and manage their emotional responses. Additionally, meditation has been shown to lower levels of cortisol, the stress hormone, in the body, which can have a positive impact on overall health and well-being.

Furthermore, meditation has been found to be an effective technique for managing symptoms of anxiety disorders, such as generalized anxiety disorder and social anxiety. By cultivating a sense of mindfulness and self-awareness through meditation, individuals can learn to observe their thoughts and feelings without reacting to them. This can help break the cycle of negative thinking and reduce the intensity of anxiety symptoms. Additionally, practicing meditation regularly can improve overall emotional regulation and resilience, making individuals less susceptible to anxiety triggers.

Another benefit of meditation is its ability to improve sleep quality and promote relaxation. Many individuals who struggle with stress and anxiety also experience difficulty sleeping, as racing thoughts and worry can interfere with the ability to fall asleep and stay asleep. Meditation can help calm the mind and release tension in the body, making it easier to relax and unwind before bedtime. By incorporating meditation into a nightly routine, individuals can create a sense of calm and prepare the mind and body for a restful night's sleep. By cultivating mindfulness and self-awareness through regular practice, individuals can create a sense of inner peace and clarity that can help them cope with the challenges of daily life. Research has shown that meditation can lead to physical changes in the brain that are associated with reduced stress and anxiety, as well as provide effective symptom management for anxiety disorders. Additionally, meditation can improve sleep quality and promote relaxation, making it a valuable tool for overall health and well-being. In today's fast-paced world, where stress and anxiety are all too common, meditation offers a natural and accessible way to find balance and cultivate a sense of inner peace.

- How meditation enhances our overall well-being

It has been proven to have numerous benefits for both the mind and body, including reducing stress, improving focus and concentration, increasing self-awareness, and promoting emotional health. By incorporating meditation into our daily routine, we can experience a greater sense of peace, happiness, and fulfillment in our lives. Stress is a common part of modern life, and can have a detrimental impact on our physical and mental health. When we experience stress, our bodies release cortisol, a hormone that can lead to a range of health problems, such as high blood pressure, heart disease, and anxiety.

In addition to reducing stress, meditation can also improve our focus and concentration. In today's fast-paced world, it can be difficult to stay present and focused on the task at hand. Our minds are constantly bombarded with distractions, making it challenging to concentrate on one thing for an extended period of time. Meditation can help to train our minds to be more focused and attentive, allowing us to be more efficient and productive in our daily lives.

Furthermore, meditation can increase our self-awareness and promote emotional health. By taking the time to sit quietly and observe our thoughts and emotions, we can develop a greater understanding of ourselves and our inner workings. This self-awareness can lead to a deeper sense of self-acceptance and self-love, as well as a greater capacity for empathy and compassion towards others. By reducing stress, improving focus and concentration, increasing self-awareness, and promoting emotional health, meditation can help us to live more balanced, fulfilling lives.

- Scientific research supporting the effectiveness of meditation

Meditation has garnered increasing attention in recent years as a powerful tool for enhancing mental and physical well-being. This article reviews the current body of scientific literature supporting the effectiveness of meditation, focusing on key research findings and their implications for individuals seeking to incorporate meditation into their daily routine.

One of the most well-documented benefits of meditation is its ability to reduce stress and promote relaxation. Numerous studies have shown that regular meditation practice can lead to a significant decrease in levels of stress hormones such as cortisol, as well as improvements in other markers of stress such as blood pressure and heart rate variability. For example, a meta-analysis published in the Journal of Psychosomatic Research found that meditation is effective in reducing symptoms of anxiety and depression, with the strongest effects seen in individuals with high levels of stress. This suggests that meditation may be particularly beneficial for those seeking relief from chronic stress or mental health conditions.

In addition to its stress-reducing effects, meditation has also been shown to improve cognitive function and enhance concentration and focus. Research has demonstrated that regular meditation practice can lead to structural changes in the brain, including increases in gray matter volume in regions associated with attention and memory. A study published in the journal Psychological Science found that just two weeks of mindfulness meditation training led to improvements in cognitive performance and working memory capacity. These findings suggest that meditation may be a valuable tool for individuals looking to boost their cognitive abilities and enhance their mental clarity. A study published in the journal Brain, Behavior, and Immunity found that mindfulness meditation training was associated with reductions in markers of inflammation and improvements in immune response in breast cancer survivors. These findings suggest that meditation may have a holistic impact on health, promoting both physical and mental well-being. These findings highlight the potential benefits of incorporating meditation into one's daily routine, whether through mindfulness practices, breathing exercises, or guided meditation sessions. As research continues to uncover the mechanisms underlying the beneficial effects of meditation, it is likely that its popularity will continue to grow as individuals seek to harness its transformative power for their own health and well-being.

Chapter 4: Getting Started with Meditation

- SIMPLE MEDITATION techniques for beginners

Meditation is a timeless practice that has been used by various cultures and traditions for centuries as a tool for promoting mental clarity, emotional well-being, and spiritual growth. For beginners looking to start their meditation journey, it can feel overwhelming and daunting to know where to begin. However, there are simple meditation techniques that can help you ease into the practice and reap its many benefits.

One of the most straightforward meditation techniques for beginners is the practice of mindfulness meditation. Mindfulness meditation involves being fully present in the moment and observing your thoughts, feelings, and sensations without judgment. To start practicing mindfulness meditation, find a comfortable and quiet place where you won't be disturbed. Sit or lie down in a relaxed position, close your eyes, and focus on your breath. Notice the sensation of your breath as it enters and leaves your body, and gently bring your attention back to your breath whenever your mind starts to wander. Start with just a few minutes of mindfulness meditation each day, gradually increasing the duration as you become more comfortable with the practice.

Another simple meditation technique for beginners is guided visualization. Guided visualization involves imagining a peaceful and calming scene in your mind's eye, such as a beach, forest, or mountain. To practice guided visualization, find a quiet and comfortable place to sit or lie down, close your eyes, and start to imagine your chosen peaceful scene in vivid detail. Focus on the sights, sounds, and sensations of the scene, allowing yourself to feel calm and relaxed. You can find guided visualization scripts online or use a meditation app that offers guided visualization sessions to help you get started.

Body scan meditation is another effective technique for beginners that can help promote relaxation and body awareness. Body scan meditation involves slowly bringing your attention to different parts of your body, starting from your toes and moving up to your head. To practice body scan meditation, find a quiet and comfortable place to sit or lie down, close your eyes, and start to bring your awareness to your toes. Notice any sensations or tension in your toes, and then slowly move your attention up to your feet, ankles, and so on, until you reach the top of your head. This practice can help you release tension and become more aware of any areas of discomfort in your body.

Breathing exercises are another simple meditation technique that can be beneficial for beginners. Deep breathing exercises help calm the mind, reduce stress, and improve focus and concentration. To practice deep breathing, find a comfortable place to sit or lie down, close your eyes, and start to take slow, deep breaths in through your nose and out through your mouth. Focus on the sensation of your breath as it enters and leaves your body, and allow yourself to relax with each exhale. You can also try counting your breaths or using a breathing exercise app to guide you through different breathing techniques. For beginners looking to start their meditation journey, there are simple techniques that can help ease them into the practice and experience its many benefits. Mindfulness meditation, guided visualization, body scan meditation, and breathing exercises are all effective techniques that beginners can try to start their meditation journey. By dedicating just a few minutes each day to these practices, beginners can cultivate a sense of calm, clarity, and inner peace in their lives.

- Tips for creating a peaceful meditation space

Creating a peaceful meditation space is essential for achieving a sense of tranquility and focus during your meditation practice. Whether you are a beginner or an experienced meditator, having a dedicated space for your practice can greatly enhance your ability to find inner peace and relaxation. In this guide, we will explore some tips for creating a peaceful meditation space that is conducive to deepening your practice and fostering a sense of calm and centeredness.

The first step in creating a peaceful meditation space is to find a quiet and secluded area in your home where you can practice without interruptions. Ideally, this space should be free from distractions such as noise, clutter, or electronic devices. Choose a room or corner of a room that is away from high-traffic areas and has minimal visual clutter. It is important to create a sense of spaciousness and simplicity in your meditation space to help cultivate a sense of peace and serenity.

Once you have found a suitable location for your meditation space, you can start to personalize it to suit your needs and preferences. Consider adding elements that evoke a sense of calm and relaxation, such as soft lighting, calming colors, and natural materials. You may also want to include items that have special significance to you, such as photos, crystals, or meaningful objects. These personal touches can help create a sense of comfort and familiarity in your space, making it easier to relax and focus during your meditation practice.

Another important aspect of creating a peaceful meditation space is to ensure that it is clean and tidy. Clutter can create a sense of chaos and distraction, which can impede your ability to focus during meditation. Take the time to clear out any unnecessary items and organize your space in a way that feels calming and harmonious. Consider using storage solutions such as baskets or shelves to keep your meditation area tidy and free from clutter.

In addition to physical elements, consider incorporating sensory elements into your meditation space to enhance your practice. For example, you may want to include relaxing scents such as incense, candles, or essential oils to create a calming atmosphere. Soft music or nature sounds can also help create a peaceful ambiance and drown out any distracting noises. Experiment with different sensory elements to find what works best for you and helps you to relax and focus during meditation.

To summarize, consider incorporating elements of nature into your meditation space to help create a sense of peace and connection with the natural world. This could be as simple as incorporating houseplants or flowers into your space, or as elaborate as creating a mini indoor garden or waterfall. Being surrounded by elements of nature can help calm your mind and create a sense of harmony and balance, making it easier to connect with your inner self during meditation. By following these tips and personalizing your space to suit your needs and preferences, you can create a sanctuary where you can relax, focus, and connect with your inner self. Remember that the most important aspect of your meditation space is that it feels calming, comfortable, and conducive to deepening your practice. Experiment with different elements and find what works best for you to create a peaceful and harmonious environment for your meditation practice.

- Overcoming common obstacles in meditation practice

Meditation is a powerful tool that can help individuals reduce stress, increase their focus, and enhance their overall well-being. However, many people encounter common obstacles that can hinder their meditation practice. By understanding these obstacles and learning how to overcome them, individuals can deepen their meditation practice and experience the full benefits it has to offer.

One common obstacle in meditation practice is a wandering mind. It is natural for thoughts to come and go during meditation, but when the mind constantly wanders, it can be challenging to stay focused. To overcome this obstacle, it is important to gently redirect the mind back to the present moment whenever it starts to wander. One helpful technique is to focus on the breath, using it as an anchor to keep the mind centered. By bringing attention back to the breath whenever thoughts arise, individuals can train their minds to stay present and focused during meditation.

Another common obstacle is discomfort or pain in the body. Sitting still for an extended period of time can lead to physical discomfort, which can be distracting during meditation. To address this obstacle, individuals can experiment with different meditation postures to find one that is comfortable for them. It is important to sit in a position that allows the body to be relaxed and at ease, whether that is sitting on a cushion, kneeling, or lying down. Additionally, incorporating movement practices such as yoga or stretching before meditation can help release tension in the body and make sitting more comfortable.

A lack of time is another obstacle that many people face when trying to establish a regular meditation practice. In today's fast-paced world, finding time for meditation can be challenging, but it is essential to prioritize self-care and make time for practices that promote well-being. To overcome this obstacle, individuals can start by setting aside just a few minutes each day for meditation, gradually increasing the length of their practice as they become more comfortable. It can also be helpful to establish a regular meditation routine, whether it is first thing in the morning, during lunch breaks, or before bed. By committing to a consistent practice, individuals can make meditation a priority in their daily lives.

Distractions are another common obstacle that can disrupt meditation practice. Whether it is external distractions such as noise or movement in the environment, or internal distractions such as racing thoughts or emotions, it can be challenging to maintain focus during meditation. To overcome distractions, individuals can create a dedicated meditation space that is quiet and free of distractions, or use earplugs or a white noise machine to block out external noise. It can also be helpful to acknowledge and observe internal distractions without attaching to them, allowing thoughts and emotions to come and go without judgment. By cultivating a sense of mindfulness and awareness, individuals can learn to navigate distractions and stay grounded in their meditation practice.

Lastly, a lack of motivation or consistency can be a major obstacle in maintaining a regular meditation practice. It is common for individuals to start off strong with meditation, only to lose momentum over time. To overcome this obstacle, it is important to set realistic goals and expectations for meditation, starting with small, achievable steps. Celebrating progress and milestones along the way can help individuals stay motivated and committed to their practice. Additionally, finding a community or support system of like-minded individuals can provide encouragement and accountability in maintaining a regular meditation routine. By cultivating a sense of discipline and dedication, individuals can overcome obstacles and continue to deepen their meditation practice over time. By understanding and addressing common obstacles such as a wandering mind, physical discomfort, lack of time, distractions, and lack of motivation, individuals can overcome these challenges and deepen their meditation practice. With patience, perseverance, and a willingness to adapt, individuals can cultivate a meditation practice that supports their overall well-being and enhances their quality of life.

Chapter 5: Mindfulness Meditation

- INTRODUCTION TO MINDFULNESS meditation

Mindfulness meditation is a practice that has been around for centuries, but has gained significant popularity in recent years due to its numerous health benefits and stress-relieving properties. It is a form of meditation that focuses on being fully present and aware of the present moment, without judgment or attachment to thoughts or emotions. This practice has its roots in ancient Buddhist traditions, but has been adapted and modernized for use in contemporary settings such as schools, workplaces, and healthcare settings.

One of the key components of mindfulness meditation is the development of self-awareness. By focusing on the breath or other sensations in the body, practitioners are able to cultivate a deeper understanding of their thoughts and emotions, and how they influence their behavior. This can lead to greater emotional intelligence, as well as improved self-regulation and resilience in the face of stress and adversity. Research has shown that regular practice of mindfulness meditation can reduce symptoms of anxiety and depression, improve attention and focus, and enhance feelings of well-being and connectedness.

Another important aspect of mindfulness meditation is the cultivation of non-judgmental awareness. This involves observing thoughts and emotions as they arise, without getting caught up in them or reacting impulsively. Instead of labeling thoughts as "good" or "bad," practitioners are encouraged to simply notice them and let them pass without attachment. This practice can help to reduce rumination and negative self-talk, and promote a more balanced and compassionate relationship with oneself.

In addition to the mental health benefits of mindfulness meditation, research has also shown that it can have positive effects on physical health. Regular practice has been associated with lower blood pressure, improved immune function, and reduced inflammation in the body. This is thought to be due to the stress-reducing effects of mindfulness meditation, which can help to decrease the production of stress hormones such as cortisol and adrenaline. By promoting relaxation and a sense of calm, mindfulness meditation may also support overall health and well-being.

While mindfulness meditation can be practiced on one's own, many people find it helpful to learn from a qualified teacher or guide. There are a variety of resources available, including books, apps, and online courses, that can provide instruction and support for those interested in starting a mindfulness meditation practice. Beginners may find it helpful to start with shorter sessions, gradually building up to longer periods of practice as they become more comfortable with the techniques. It is also important to approach mindfulness meditation with an open mind and a spirit of curiosity, as it is a practice that can evolve and deepen over time. By cultivating self-awareness, non-judgmental awareness, and a sense of calm, practitioners can experience greater emotional intelligence, reduced stress, and improved overall health. With regular practice and dedication, mindfulness meditation can become a valuable part of one's daily routine, providing a sense of peace and clarity in an increasingly busy and fast-paced world.

- Techniques for staying present and focused

In today's fast-paced world, staying present and focused can be a challenging task. With constant distractions from technology, work, and personal responsibilities, it can be easy to feel overwhelmed and unfocused. However, there are several techniques that can help individuals stay present and focused in their daily lives.

One technique that can be useful in staying present and focused is mindfulness meditation. Mindfulness meditation involves focusing on the present moment and observing your thoughts and feelings without judgment. By practicing mindfulness meditation regularly, individuals can train their minds to be more present and focused in their daily lives. This can help individuals stay focused on the task at hand and prevent their minds from wandering to other distractions.

Another technique that can help individuals stay present and focused is setting clear goals and priorities. By setting specific goals and priorities for each day, individuals can stay focused on what is most important and prevent themselves from becoming overwhelmed with multiple tasks. By prioritizing tasks and focusing on one thing at a time, individuals can stay present in the moment and give their full attention to the task at hand.

In addition to setting clear goals and priorities, it can be helpful to establish a daily routine that incorporates time for rest and relaxation. By taking breaks throughout the day and engaging in activities that help individuals relax and recharge, they can maintain their focus and stay present in the moment. This can include taking short walks, practicing deep breathing exercises, or engaging in a hobby that brings joy and relaxation.

Furthermore, technology can be a major source of distraction in today's world. To stay present and focused, individuals can set boundaries with technology use and establish specific times for checking emails, social media, and other notifications. By limiting technology use and setting aside designated times for checking devices, individuals can reduce distractions and stay focused on the task at hand.

Another technique for staying present and focused is practicing gratitude. By focusing on the present moment and expressing gratitude for the things in one's life, individuals can cultivate a positive mindset and stay focused on the present moment. Gratitude practices can include keeping a gratitude journal, expressing gratitude to others, or simply taking a few moments each day to reflect on what is going well in one's life. However, by implementing techniques such as mindfulness meditation, setting clear goals and priorities, establishing a daily routine, setting boundaries with technology use, and practicing gratitude, individuals can stay present and focused in their daily lives. By making a conscious effort to prioritize staying present and focused, individuals can enhance their productivity, reduce stress, and experience greater satisfaction and fulfillment in their daily lives.

- Practicing mindfulness in everyday life

Mindfulness is a practice that has gained significant popularity in recent years as a tool for managing stress, increasing self-awareness, and enhancing overall well-being. While mindfulness has its roots in Buddhism, it has been adapted and secularized for a Western audience, making it accessible to people from all backgrounds. The concept of mindfulness revolves around being fully present in the moment, paying attention to your thoughts and feelings without judgment, and cultivating a sense of awareness and acceptance. By practicing mindfulness in everyday life, individuals can experience a host of benefits, including reduced anxiety and depression, improved focus and concentration, and greater emotional resilience.

One of the key principles of mindfulness is the idea of being fully present in the moment. In today's fast-paced society, it is all too easy to get caught up in the hustle and bustle of daily life, constantly rushing from one task to the next without taking the time to pause and appreciate the present moment. Mindfulness encourages individuals to slow down and pay attention to their thoughts, feelings, and sensations, allowing them to fully engage with the present moment and experience life more fully. By practicing mindfulness in everyday life, individuals can become more aware of the present moment and cultivate a sense of gratitude for the simple pleasures that life has to offer.

Another important aspect of mindfulness is the practice of paying attention to your thoughts and feelings without judgment. Many of us are quick to label our thoughts as "good" or "bad," "positive" or "negative," which can lead to a cycle of self-criticism and self-doubt. Mindfulness teaches individuals to observe their thoughts and feelings with curiosity and compassion, without getting caught up in self-judgment. By learning to approach their thoughts with a sense of openness and acceptance, individuals can gain a more balanced perspective on their inner experiences and develop a greater sense of self-compassion.

Practicing mindfulness in everyday life can also help individuals improve their focus and concentration. In a world filled with distractions and constant stimulus, it is easy to become overwhelmed and lose sight of our priorities. Mindfulness teaches individuals to focus their attention on the present moment, letting go of distractions and unnecessary worries. By training the mind to be more present and focused, individuals can enhance their productivity and performance in various areas of their life, whether it be at work, in relationships, or during leisure activities.

Furthermore, mindfulness can help individuals develop greater emotional resilience in the face of life's challenges. By cultivating a sense of awareness and acceptance of their thoughts and feelings, individuals can learn to respond to difficult situations with greater equanimity and clarity. Instead of reacting impulsively to stress or adversity, individuals can take a step back, tune into their inner experiences, and choose a more skillful response. This ability to stay grounded in the present moment and regulate one's emotions can help individuals navigate life's ups and downs with greater ease and grace. By being fully present in the moment, paying attention to one's thoughts and feelings without judgment, and improving focus and concentration, individuals can enhance their overall well-being and quality of life. Mindfulness is not a one-size-fits-all approach, and it may take time and practice to incorporate into one's daily routine. However, with patience and dedication, individuals can cultivate a greater sense of awareness, clarity, and compassion in their lives, leading to a deeper sense of fulfillment and happiness.

Chapter 6: Loving-Kindness Meditation

- UNDERSTANDING LOVING-kindness meditation

Loving-kindness meditation, also known as Metta meditation, is a practice rooted in Buddhist traditions that focuses on cultivating feelings of love, compassion, and goodwill towards oneself and others. This form of meditation involves directing positive emotions and intentions towards oneself, loved ones, acquaintances, difficult individuals, and all beings in the world. The primary goal of loving-kindness meditation is to foster a sense of interconnectedness, empathy, and kindness towards all living beings, ultimately leading to a more peaceful and loving outlook on life.

One of the key components of loving-kindness meditation is the cultivation of loving-kindness towards oneself. Often, individuals are harsh and critical towards themselves, leading to feelings of low self-worth and unhappiness. Through loving-kindness meditation, practitioners learn to treat themselves with the same kindness and compassion they would offer to a close friend or family member. This practice involves repeating phrases such as "May I be happy, may I be healthy, may I be safe, may I live with ease" while focusing on feelings of warmth and unconditional love towards oneself.

In addition to self-love, loving-kindness meditation also involves extending these feelings of kindness and compassion towards others. Practitioners typically start by directing loving-kindness towards loved ones, such as family members, friends, and mentors. As they become more skilled in the practice, they can also extend these feelings towards acquaintances, strangers, and even difficult individuals in their lives. By cultivating feelings of love and compassion towards all beings, practitioners strive to break free from feelings of anger, resentment, and judgment, ultimately fostering a greater sense of unity and harmony with the world around them.

One of the distinguishing features of loving-kindness meditation is its emphasis on the universality of love and compassion. Unlike other forms of meditation that may focus on the individual's personal growth and well-being, loving-kindness meditation emphasizes the interconnectedness of all living beings. By recognizing that all beings share a common desire for happiness and freedom from suffering, practitioners develop a sense of empathy and compassion that transcends individual boundaries. This universal outlook promotes a sense of unity and interconnectedness with all beings, leading to a deeper sense of peace and contentment.

While loving-kindness meditation has its roots in Buddhist traditions, it is a practice that can be adapted and integrated into various spiritual and secular contexts. The core principles of loving-kindness – love, compassion, empathy, and interconnectedness – resonate with individuals from diverse backgrounds and belief systems. Whether practiced as part of a formal meditation routine or incorporated into daily life through acts of kindness and compassion, loving-kindness meditation offers a powerful tool for cultivating a more loving and harmonious relationship with oneself and others. By cultivating feelings of love, compassion, and goodwill towards oneself and others, practitioners can break free from negative emotions such as anger, resentment, and judgment, leading to a greater sense of peace, happiness, and interconnectedness with all beings. Whether practiced as a formal meditation routine or integrated into daily life through acts of kindness and compassion, loving-kindness meditation offers a powerful and accessible way to cultivate a more loving and harmonious way of being in the world.

- Cultivating compassion and empathy through meditation

As humans, we are inherently wired to connect with others and experience feelings of compassion and empathy. These qualities are essential for building strong relationships, fostering understanding, and promoting a sense of community. However, in today's fast-paced world, it can be easy to lose sight of our capacity for compassion and empathy as we become consumed by our own needs and desires. This is where the practice of meditation can be truly transformative.

Meditation is a powerful tool that can help us cultivate compassion and empathy by allowing us to quiet our minds and become more in tune with our emotions and the emotions of others. Through regular meditation practice, we can learn to be more present in the moment and develop a greater sense of self-awareness. This heightened awareness can help us recognize when we are feeling closed off or disconnected from others, allowing us to shift our focus towards cultivating feelings of compassion and empathy instead.

One of the key components of cultivating compassion and empathy through meditation is learning to practice loving-kindness meditation. This type of meditation involves sending feelings of love, kindness, and compassion to ourselves and others. By practicing loving-kindness meditation, we can train our minds to see the inherent goodness in ourselves and others, and cultivate a sense of connection and understanding that transcends our own self-interest.

Another important aspect of cultivating compassion and empathy through meditation is developing mindfulness. Mindfulness involves paying attention to the present moment with a non-judgmental and accepting attitude. By practicing mindfulness meditation, we can cultivate a greater sense of empathy by being fully present with the emotions of others and responding to them with kindness and understanding. This can help us build stronger relationships and foster a greater sense of connection with those around us.

In addition to loving-kindness and mindfulness meditation, cultivating compassion and empathy through meditation can also involve practicing gratitude. Gratitude meditation involves reflecting on the things we are grateful for in our lives and cultivating a sense of appreciation for the kindness and generosity of others. By practicing gratitude meditation, we can increase our capacity for compassion and empathy by recognizing the interconnectedness of all living beings and cultivating a sense of empathy and understanding for the struggles and suffering of others.

Ultimately, cultivating compassion and empathy through meditation is about developing a deeper sense of connection with ourselves and others. By regularly practicing meditation, we can train our minds to be more aware of our emotions and the emotions of others, and respond to them with kindness and understanding. This can help us build stronger relationships, foster a greater sense of empathy, and create a more compassionate and empathetic world for all.

- How loving-kindness meditation improves relationships and reduces negative emotions

Loving-kindness meditation, also known as Mettā meditation, is a practice rooted in Buddhist traditions that focuses on cultivating feelings of love, compassion, and kindness towards oneself and others. This form of meditation has gained popularity in recent years as a powerful tool for improving relationships and reducing negative emotions. Research has shown that engaging in loving-kindness meditation can have a profound impact on one's emotional well-being and interpersonal connections.

One of the key ways in which loving-kindness meditation improves relationships is by fostering a greater sense of empathy and compassion towards others. By regularly practicing mettā meditation, individuals learn to cultivate feelings of love and kindness towards themselves and extend these feelings towards others. This shift in mindset can lead to a more positive outlook on life and a greater sense of connection with those around us. As a result, individuals are more likely to approach their relationships with an open heart and a willingness to understand and support others in their journey.

Another way in which loving-kindness meditation enhances relationships is by helping individuals develop a greater sense of emotional regulation and resilience. Negative emotions such as anger, resentment, and jealousy can often cloud our judgment and lead to conflicts in our relationships. By practicing loving-kindness meditation, individuals learn to acknowledge and accept these challenging emotions without getting caught up in them. This increased emotional awareness allows individuals to respond to difficult situations with greater compassion and understanding, rather than reacting impulsively with negativity. As a result, conflicts are less likely to escalate, and relationships are more likely to thrive.

Furthermore, loving-kindness meditation has been shown to improve communication skills and increase feelings of trust and intimacy within relationships. When individuals practice mettā meditation, they develop a greater capacity for active listening and effective communication. By approaching interactions with an attitude of kindness and understanding, individuals create an atmosphere of mutual respect and empathy in their relationships. This, in turn, fosters a sense of trust and intimacy between individuals, allowing for deeper connections and stronger bonds to form.

In addition to improving relationships, loving-kindness meditation has been found to reduce negative emotions such as anxiety, stress, and depression. By cultivating feelings of love and kindness towards oneself and others, individuals can counteract the harmful effects of negative emotions on their mental and emotional well-being. Regular practice of mettā meditation has been shown to increase feelings of happiness and contentment, while reducing symptoms of anxiety and depression. This can have a significant impact on one's overall quality of life and ability to navigate the challenges of daily living with greater resilience and ease. By fostering a sense of empathy, emotional regulation, and trust within relationships, individuals can experience greater connection and intimacy with others. Furthermore, by managing negative emotions and cultivating feelings of love and kindness, individuals can experience a greater sense of well-being and happiness in their lives. It is clear that loving-kindness meditation has the potential to create positive changes in our relationships and emotional well-being, making it a valuable tool for personal growth and development.

Chapter 7: Body Scan Meditation

- BENEFITS OF BODY SCAN meditation for relaxation and stress reduction

Meditation is a practice that has been utilized for centuries as a means of achieving relaxation, mental clarity, and stress reduction. One form of meditation that has gained popularity in recent years is body scan meditation. This technique involves systematically focusing on different parts of the body, becoming aware of any sensations or tensions present, and then releasing them through deep breathing and mindful attention.

The benefits of body scan meditation for relaxation and stress reduction are numerous and well-documented. One of the primary advantages of this practice is its ability to increase mindfulness and body awareness. By directing attention to different regions of the body, individuals can become more attuned to physical sensations and recognize areas of tension or discomfort that they may not have been aware of before. This heightened awareness can help them address and release these tensions, leading to a greater sense of relaxation and well-being.

Additionally, body scan meditation is an effective method for reducing stress and anxiety. Research has shown that stress can manifest in the body as physical tension, which can further exacerbate feelings of anxiety and unease. By systematically scanning the body and releasing tension through deep breathing and relaxation techniques, individuals can reduce overall stress levels and promote a sense of calm and tranquility.

Furthermore, body scan meditation can also improve sleep quality and promote better overall health. Many individuals who struggle with stress and anxiety also experience sleep disturbances, such as insomnia or restlessness. By practicing body scan meditation before bedtime, individuals can relax their bodies and minds, promoting a more restful and rejuvenating sleep. This, in turn, can lead to improved mood, energy levels, and overall well-being.

In addition to its physical and mental benefits, body scan meditation can also enhance emotional well-being and self-awareness. By tuning into different sensations and emotions present in the body, individuals can cultivate a greater sense of self-awareness and emotional intelligence. This can help them better navigate challenging situations, manage emotions effectively, and enhance their overall sense of well-being and resilience.

Moreover, body scan meditation is a versatile practice that can be easily incorporated into daily life. Whether practiced for a few minutes before bed, during a break at work, or as part of a morning routine, body scan meditation can be a simple and accessible tool for promoting relaxation and stress reduction. Its flexibility and ease of application make it an ideal practice for individuals looking to integrate mindfulness and self-care into their daily lives. By increasing mindfulness and body awareness, reducing stress and anxiety, improving sleep quality, promoting emotional well-being, and enhancing self-awareness, this practice can be a powerful tool for enhancing overall well-being. Its accessibility and versatility make it a valuable addition to any wellness routine, offering individuals a simple yet effective way to cultivate a sense of peace, balance, and vitality in their lives.

- Steps for practicing a body scan meditation

Body scan meditation is a powerful technique that can help individuals cultivate mindfulness, reduce stress, and improve overall well-being. This practice involves systematically focusing on different parts of the body, bringing awareness to physical sensations and promoting relaxation. While body scan meditation may seem simple on the surface, there are several steps that can help individuals make the most of their practice.

The first step in practicing a body scan meditation is to find a quiet and comfortable space where you can sit or lie down without distractions. It is important to create a peaceful environment where you can fully focus on the sensations in your body. You may choose to dim the lights, play calming music, or use a guided meditation recording to help you stay present and relaxed.

Once you have found a comfortable position, begin by taking a few deep breaths to center yourself and bring your awareness to the present moment. Start by focusing on your breath, noticing the sensations of inhalation and exhalation as you breathe in and out. Allow yourself to fully experience each breath, letting go of any thoughts or distractions that may arise.

Next, slowly shift your attention to different parts of your body, starting at your toes and working your way up to the top of your head. As you focus on each body part, take a moment to notice any sensations or feelings that arise. Pay attention to any areas of tension, discomfort, or relaxation, without trying to change or fix anything. Simply observe and accept whatever you are feeling in the present moment.

As you move through each body part, continue to breathe deeply and maintain a sense of curiosity and openness. Try to approach each sensation with a nonjudgmental attitude, allowing yourself to experience whatever arises without attaching to it or trying to control it. Remember that the goal of body scan meditation is not to "fix" anything, but rather to cultivate a sense of awareness and acceptance of the present moment.

If you find your mind wandering or becoming distracted during the practice, gently guide your attention back to your breath and the body part you are focusing on. It is natural for thoughts to come and go, but the key is to gently redirect your focus without judgment or frustration. Remember that each moment of awareness is an opportunity to deepen your practice and cultivate mindfulness.

Ultimately, as you reach the end of the body scan meditation, take a few moments to reflect on your experience and how you are feeling. Notice any changes in your physical sensations, emotions, or overall sense of well-being. Allow yourself to savor the feelings of relaxation and peace that may have emerged during the practice. Take a few more deep breaths before slowly returning to the present moment, feeling grounded and centered in your body. By following these steps and practicing regularly, individuals can develop a deeper awareness of their bodies, reduce stress, and improve their overall well-being. Remember that each meditation session is a unique experience, and there is no "right" or "wrong" way to practice. The key is to approach the practice with an open mind, compassion, and a willingness to be present in the moment. With dedication and patience, body scan meditation can become a valuable part of your self-care routine and help you navigate life with greater ease and awareness.

- Physical and emotional sensations to pay attention to during a body scan

A body scan is a mindfulness technique that involves focusing on different parts of the body, from head to toe, to bring awareness to physical sensations, thoughts, and emotions. It is an effective tool for reducing stress, anxiety, and tension in the body. During a body scan, it is important to pay attention to both physical and emotional sensations as they can provide valuable insights into the state of your mind and body.

When engaging in a body scan, it is essential to be aware of any physical sensations that arise. This includes sensations of tension, tightness, pain, warmth, or tingling in different parts of the body. By paying attention to these physical sensations, you can identify areas of the body that may be holding onto stress or tension. For example, if you notice tightness in your shoulders or a headache forming, this may be a sign that you are carrying stress in those areas and need to take steps to release it.

In addition to physical sensations, it is crucial to also be mindful of any emotional sensations that arise during a body scan. This includes feelings of anxiety, sadness, joy, anger, or any other emotional state that may come up. Emotions are often stored in the body and can manifest as physical sensations. For example, feelings of sadness may be felt as a heaviness in the chest, while anxiety may be felt as a knot in the stomach. By paying attention to these emotional sensations, you can gain insight into your emotional state and address any underlying issues that may be causing them.

One important aspect of a body scan is to approach it with a non-judgmental attitude. This means observing both physical and emotional sensations without attaching any labels or judgments to them. Instead of labeling sensations as good or bad, simply observe them as they are and let them pass without becoming attached to them. This can help you cultivate a sense of mindfulness and self-compassion, which are essential for reducing stress and promoting emotional well-being.

During a body scan, it can be helpful to use different techniques to guide your attention to different parts of the body. For example, you can start by focusing on the sensations in your toes, then gradually work your way up to your head, paying attention to each body part along the way. You can also use visualization techniques, such as imagining a warm light or relaxing sensation moving through your body, to help deepen your awareness of physical and emotional sensations. So next time you engage in a body scan, take the time to be present with both your physical and emotional sensations, and observe how they can provide valuable insights into your state of mind and body.

Chapter 8: Guided Imagery Meditation

- USING GUIDED IMAGERY to calm the mind and reduce anxiety

Guided imagery is a powerful and effective technique that can be used to calm the mind and reduce anxiety. It involves using mental imagery to create a calming and relaxing mental state. This technique has been widely used in therapy and mindfulness practices to help individuals manage stress and anxiety. By guiding the mind through soothing and peaceful images, individuals are able to shift their focus away from their worries and fears, and instead, create a sense of peace and relaxation.

One of the key reasons why guided imagery is effective in reducing anxiety is because it helps to activate the body's relaxation response. When we experience stress and anxiety, our body goes into a state of high alert, with the fight-or-flight response kicking in. This response triggers the release of stress hormones like cortisol and adrenaline, which can have a negative impact on our physical and mental health. Guided imagery helps to counteract this response by activating the body's relaxation response, which promotes the release of calming neurotransmitters and reduces the production of stress hormones. This can help to lower blood pressure, slow heart rate, and promote a sense of peace and well-being.

In addition to activating the relaxation response, guided imagery can also help individuals to develop greater self-awareness and mindfulness. By guiding the mind through calming and relaxing images, individuals are able to become more aware of their thoughts and emotions, and learn to observe them without judgment. This can help individuals to develop a greater sense of self-control and emotional regulation, and reduce the tendency to get caught up in negative thinking patterns. By cultivating mindfulness through guided imagery, individuals can learn to respond to stressful situations with greater calmness and clarity, rather than reacting impulsively out of fear or anxiety.

Another key benefit of guided imagery is its ability to harness the power of the mind to create positive change. Our thoughts and beliefs have a powerful impact on our emotions and behaviors. By using guided imagery to focus on positive and soothing images, individuals can reframe their thoughts and beliefs in more positive and empowering ways. This can help to reduce the grip of negative thinking patterns and replace them with more positive and affirming beliefs. By repeatedly engaging in guided imagery exercises, individuals can create new neural pathways in the brain that support a more positive and peaceful mental state.

Guided imagery is a versatile technique that can be easily incorporated into daily routines to promote relaxation and reduce anxiety. It can be practiced in a variety of ways, including through guided meditation recordings, visualization exercises, or even through simple mental exercises. One of the key principles of guided imagery is the use of all five senses to create a vivid and immersive mental experience. By engaging all of the senses in the imagery, individuals can create a more vibrant and realistic experience that can help to deepen relaxation and promote a sense of well-being.

It is important to note that guided imagery is not a cure-all for anxiety, and may not be effective for everyone. It is always important to consult with a mental health professional before trying any new relaxation or mindfulness technique, especially if you have a history of mental health issues. That being said, guided imagery can be a valuable tool in managing anxiety and promoting relaxation. By harnessing the power of the mind to create positive change, individuals can cultivate greater self-awareness, mindfulness, and emotional regulation, and develop a greater sense of peace and well-being.

- Visualizing positive and peaceful scenes during meditation

Visualizing positive and peaceful scenes during meditation is a common practice that is believed to help individuals relax, focus their minds, and reduce stress. This technique involves creating mental images of serene and tranquil settings, such as a peaceful beach or a lush forest, to help calm the mind and promote a sense of well-being. By actively engaging in this form of visualization, individuals can shift their focus away from negative thoughts and emotions, and instead cultivate feelings of positivity and inner peace.

The process of visualizing positive and peaceful scenes during meditation can be a powerful tool for managing stress and anxiety. When we are faced with challenging situations or overwhelming emotions, our minds can become cluttered with negative thoughts and feelings. By taking the time to practice visualization techniques, we can redirect our attention to more calming and uplifting images, allowing us to relax and unwind. This shift in focus can help to reduce feelings of tension and anxiety, and promote a more peaceful and centered state of mind.

One of the key benefits of visualizing positive and peaceful scenes during meditation is its ability to promote a sense of relaxation and mental clarity. By immersing ourselves in peaceful imagery, we can create a mental escape from the busyness and chaos of everyday life. This can help us to unwind and de-stress, allowing us to recharge and rejuvenate our minds and bodies. In addition, this practice can help to improve our ability to concentrate and focus, by training our minds to stay present and centered on positive thoughts and images.

Another important aspect of visualizing positive and peaceful scenes during meditation is its ability to enhance our emotional well-being. By focusing on uplifting and calming images, we can cultivate feelings of joy, contentment, and inner peace. This can help us to cultivate a more positive outlook on life, and foster a greater sense of emotional balance and resilience. In addition, by practicing visualization techniques regularly, we can develop a more positive mindset and become better equipped to handle difficult emotions and situations with grace and composure.

It is important to note that the practice of visualizing positive and peaceful scenes during meditation is a highly personal and individualized process. What works for one person may not necessarily work for another, and it is important to experiment with different techniques and approaches to find what resonates with you personally. Some individuals may find it helpful to visualize specific scenes or settings, such as a peaceful mountain retreat or a tranquil garden, while others may prefer to focus on abstract images or colors. The key is to find what brings you a sense of calm and peace, and to practice regularly to reap the benefits of this powerful technique. By taking the time to engage in this practice regularly, individuals can cultivate a more peaceful and centered state of mind, and develop a greater sense of emotional balance and resilience. Whether you are new to meditation or have been practicing for years, incorporating visualization techniques into your routine can help you to deepen your practice and experience greater levels of inner peace and well-being. Ultimately, the practice of visualizing positive and peaceful scenes during meditation is a simple yet powerful way to create a sanctuary of peace and tranquility within your own mind.

- Incorporating guided imagery into a regular meditation practice

Guided imagery is a powerful technique that can enhance and deepen one's meditation practice. By incorporating guided imagery into a regular meditation routine, individuals can tap into the power of their imagination to explore and transform their inner landscape. This practice involves using visualizations and mental imagery to create a sense of peace, relaxation, and focus during meditation. Guided imagery can help individuals connect with their emotions, thoughts, and physical sensations in a profound and meaningful way.

One of the key benefits of incorporating guided imagery into a regular meditation practice is that it can help individuals relax and reduce stress. When we engage in guided imagery, we are able to create a mental picture of a peaceful and serene place, such as a beach or a meadow, and immerse ourselves in that environment. This can help us let go of our worries and anxieties, and enter a state of deep relaxation. By focusing on calming images and sensations, we can quiet our minds and bodies, allowing us to experience a sense of peace and tranquility.

In addition to reducing stress, guided imagery can also help individuals improve their focus and concentration during meditation. When we engage in visualizations and mental imagery, we are exercising our ability to concentrate and maintain attention on a specific object or image. By practicing guided imagery regularly, individuals can enhance their ability to stay present and focused during meditation, allowing them to deepen their practice and experience greater levels of mindfulness.

Furthermore, incorporating guided imagery into a regular meditation practice can help individuals explore and process their emotions in a safe and supportive way. Through visualizations and mental imagery, individuals can tap into their inner world and connect with their feelings and emotions on a deeper level. This can help individuals gain insight into their inner workings and develop a greater sense of self-awareness. By exploring and processing their emotions through guided imagery, individuals can work through any emotional blockages or traumas they may be experiencing, leading to greater emotional well-being and healing.

Another benefit of incorporating guided imagery into a regular meditation practice is that it can help individuals cultivate a greater sense of creativity and inspiration. When we engage in guided imagery, we are opening ourselves up to the vast realm of our imagination, allowing us to explore new ideas, perspectives, and possibilities. This can help individuals break free from limiting beliefs and patterns of thinking, and tap into their creative potential. By practicing guided imagery regularly, individuals can stimulate their creativity and innovation, leading to new insights and solutions to life's challenges. By incorporating guided imagery into a regular routine, individuals can relax, reduce stress, improve focus and concentration, explore and process their emotions, and cultivate greater creativity and inspiration. Guided imagery offers a powerful way to connect with our inner world and tap into the transformative power of our imagination. By incorporating guided imagery into our meditation practice, we can expand our awareness, deepen our self-understanding, and cultivate a greater sense of peace, well-being, and inner harmony.

Chapter 9: Progressive Muscle Relaxation

- TECHNIQUE FOR RELEASING tension and stress in the body

As we navigate through the demands and challenges of modern life, it is not uncommon for our bodies to accumulate tension and stress. This can manifest in various ways, such as muscle tightness, headaches, and overall feelings of discomfort. It is essential to address these physical manifestations of stress, as they can have a significant impact on our overall well-being and quality of life. Fortunately, there are various techniques that can help release tension and stress in the body, promoting relaxation and rejuvenation.

One effective technique for releasing tension and stress in the body is progressive muscle relaxation. This technique involves systematically tensing and then relaxing different muscle groups in the body. By intentionally contracting and releasing tension in specific areas, individuals can increase their awareness of bodily sensations and promote relaxation. Progressive muscle relaxation can be done in a seated or lying down position, making it accessible and convenient for individuals of all ages and fitness levels.

To practice progressive muscle relaxation, begin by finding a quiet and comfortable space where you can relax without distractions. Start by taking a few deep breaths to center yourself and bring your awareness to your body. Then, focus on one muscle group at a time, starting with your toes and working your way up through your body. As you tense each muscle group for a few seconds, pay attention to the sensation of tension and then release the tension slowly, allowing the muscle to relax completely. Continue this process until you have tensed and relaxed each major muscle group in your body.

Another effective technique for releasing tension and stress in the body is deep breathing exercises. Deep breathing is a simple and powerful way to calm the nervous system and promote relaxation. By focusing on slow, deep breaths, individuals can increase oxygen flow to the brain and muscles, leading to a sense of calm and well-being. Deep breathing exercises can be done anywhere and at any time, making them a convenient tool for managing stress in everyday life.

To practice deep breathing, find a comfortable position and close your eyes if you feel comfortable doing so. Place one hand on your chest and the other on your abdomen. Take a deep breath in through your nose, feeling your abdomen rise as you fill your lungs with air. Hold the breath for a few seconds, then exhale slowly through your mouth, feeling your abdomen fall as you release the breath. Continue this cycle of deep breathing for several minutes, focusing on the sensation of air moving in and out of your body. With each breath, allow yourself to let go of tension and stress, creating space for relaxation and calm.

In addition to progressive muscle relaxation and deep breathing exercises, another technique for releasing tension and stress in the body is mindfulness meditation. Mindfulness meditation involves bringing your awareness to the present moment without judgment, allowing you to observe your thoughts, feelings, and bodily sensations with clarity and compassion. By practicing mindfulness meditation regularly, individuals can cultivate a sense of peace and equanimity, reducing the impact of stress on the body and mind.

To practice mindfulness meditation, find a quiet and comfortable space where you can sit or lie down. Close your eyes and bring your attention to your breath, noticing the sensation of air moving in and out of your body. As thoughts or distractions arise, gently acknowledge them and then return your focus to your breath. Allow yourself to be fully present in the moment, embracing whatever sensations or emotions arise without trying to change or control them. With regular practice, mindfulness meditation can help release tension and stress in the body, fostering a sense of balance and well-being. Whether through progressive muscle relaxation, deep breathing exercises, mindfulness meditation, or other relaxation techniques, individuals can cultivate a sense of calm and well-being, even amidst the challenges of modern life. By incorporating these practices into daily routines, individuals can support their physical and mental health, promoting resilience and vitality in the face of stress. Remember that self-care is essential for overall well-being, and taking the time to release tension and stress in the body is a powerful way to nurture and support yourself.

- Guided steps for progressive muscle relaxation

Progressive muscle relaxation (PMR) is a well-established technique that has been proven to effectively reduce muscle tension and promote relaxation in individuals. Developed by American physician Edmund Jacobson in the early 20th century, PMR involves the systematic tensing and relaxing of various muscle groups in the body. By practicing PMR regularly, individuals can learn to recognize and release muscle tension, leading to a greater sense of calm and well-being.

To begin practicing PMR, find a quiet and comfortable space where you will not be disturbed. It is recommended to practice PMR lying down, but sitting in a comfortable chair is also acceptable. Close your eyes and take a few deep breaths, focusing on slowing down your breathing and allowing your body to relax. Once you have reached a state of calm, you can begin the progressive muscle relaxation exercise.

Start by focusing on the muscles in your feet. Slowly curl your toes and tense the muscles in your feet for a few seconds, then release and allow the tension to melt away. Move on to your calves, tightening the muscles in your lower legs and then releasing. Continue this process, moving slowly up through each muscle group in your body, including your thighs, buttocks, abdomen, chest, back, arms, hands, neck, and face. Remember to focus on each muscle group individually, tensing for a few seconds before releasing and letting go of any remaining tension.

As you progress through the muscle groups, pay attention to the sensations in your body. Notice the difference between tension and relaxation, and try to fully relax each muscle group before moving on to the next. It is normal to experience some discomfort or stiffness in certain muscles, especially if you are not used to practicing PMR regularly. Take your time and be patient with yourself as you work through the exercise.

Once you have completed the progressive muscle relaxation exercise, take a few moments to sit quietly and notice how your body feels. You may feel more relaxed, light, and at ease than before you started. It is important to practice

PMR regularly, ideally daily, to experience the full benefits of the technique. Over time, you will likely notice a reduction in muscle tension, an increase in overall relaxation, and an improved sense of well-being.

In addition to practicing PMR on your own, there are many guided resources available to help you learn and master the technique. Guided PMR recordings can be found online or in various relaxation and mindfulness apps. These recordings typically walk you through the progressive muscle relaxation exercise, providing instructions and cues for each muscle group. They can be a helpful tool for beginners or individuals who prefer a more structured approach to relaxation. By practicing PMR regularly and incorporating it into your daily routine, you can learn to recognize and release muscle tension, leading to a greater sense of calm and relaxation. Remember to find a quiet and comfortable space, focus on each muscle group individually, and be patient with yourself as you work through the exercise. With practice and dedication, you can experience the many benefits of progressive muscle relaxation and enjoy a more relaxed and peaceful state of mind.

- Benefits of regular practice for overall relaxation and well-being

Regular practice of relaxation techniques has been shown to have numerous benefits for overall well-being. Whether it's through activities like meditation, yoga, tai chi, or deep breathing exercises, incorporating these practices into your daily routine can have a profound impact on your physical, mental, and emotional health. By taking the time to intentionally relax and focus on calming your mind and body, you can reduce stress, improve sleep quality, boost your immune system, and enhance your overall sense of well-being.

One of the primary benefits of regular relaxation practice is stress reduction. In today's fast-paced world, it's easy to feel overwhelmed and overburdened by the demands of daily life. Chronic stress can have serious negative effects on both your physical and mental health, leading to conditions like high blood pressure, heart disease, anxiety, and depression. By making time for relaxation each day, you can lower your stress levels and give your body a chance to rest and rejuvenate. This can help improve your mood, increase your energy levels, and enhance your ability to cope with the challenges of daily life.

In addition to reducing stress, regular relaxation practice can also improve your sleep quality. Many people struggle to get a good night's sleep due to racing thoughts, muscle tension, and overall restlessness. By incorporating relaxation techniques into your bedtime routine, you can calm your mind and body, making it easier to fall asleep and stay asleep throughout the night. Deep breathing exercises, guided imagery, and progressive muscle relaxation are all effective tools for promoting relaxation and improving sleep quality. By getting the restful sleep your body needs, you can wake up feeling refreshed and ready to face the day ahead.

Furthermore, regular relaxation practice can boost your immune system and help protect you from illness. When your body is under constant stress, your immune system can become compromised, making you more susceptible to infections and diseases. By taking the time to relax and unwind, you can give your immune system a much-needed break and help it function at its best. Research has shown that relaxation techniques like meditation and yoga can help reduce inflammation in the body, strengthen immune function, and improve overall health. By making relaxation a priority in your daily life, you can support your body's natural defenses and enhance your ability to stay healthy and well.

Another benefit of regular relaxation practice is improved mental clarity and focus. When your mind is constantly racing with thoughts and worries, it can be difficult to concentrate on tasks and make decisions. By practicing relaxation techniques regularly, you can quiet your mind and enhance your ability to focus on the present moment. Meditation, in particular, has been shown to enhance cognitive function, increase attention span, and improve memory. By making time for relaxation each day, you can sharpen your mental acuity, boost your productivity, and enhance your overall performance in work and daily activities. By reducing stress, improving sleep quality, boosting immune function, and enhancing mental clarity, these practices can help you feel more relaxed, rejuvenated, and resilient in the face of life's challenges. Whether you choose to incorporate meditation, yoga, tai chi, or deep breathing exercises into your daily routine, taking the time to relax and focus on calming your mind and body can have lasting benefits for your health and happiness. So why not give it a try and see for yourself how regular relaxation practice can improve your overall well-being.

Chapter 10: Breathwork Meditation

- IMPORTANCE OF BREATHWORK in meditation practice

Breathwork is a fundamental aspect of meditation practice, serving as a powerful tool to deepen one's mindfulness and presence in the present moment. Through intentional and conscious breathing techniques, individuals can cultivate a heightened awareness of their inner experience and establish a sense of calm and balance within themselves.

One of the primary reasons why breathwork is so essential in meditation practice is its ability to regulate the nervous system and induce a state of relaxation. By paying attention to the breath and consciously controlling its rhythm, individuals can activate the parasympathetic nervous system, which is responsible for promoting a sense of calm and reducing stress levels. This activation of the parasympathetic nervous system plays a crucial role in creating a conducive environment for meditation, allowing the mind to quieten and the body to relax, thus facilitating a deeper state of introspection and self-awareness.

Furthermore, breathwork serves as a bridge between the mind and body, helping individuals to cultivate a deeper connection to their physical and emotional experiences. Through mindful breathing, individuals can develop a greater awareness of their bodily sensations and emotional states, allowing them to navigate and process their inner landscape with greater clarity and understanding. This integration of the mind and body is essential for a holistic approach to meditation practice, as it enables individuals to access a deeper level of self-awareness and self-compassion.

In addition to its calming and grounding effects, breathwork also plays a vital role in increasing the efficiency and effectiveness of meditation practice. By bringing attention to the breath, individuals can anchor their awareness in the present moment, thus reducing the tendency of the mind to wander and get lost in thoughts. This focused attention on the breath helps individuals to cultivate a sense of presence and mindfulness, enabling them to stay present with whatever arises during meditation practice. Ultimately, by honing their ability to remain focused and attentive, individuals can deepen their meditation practice and access deeper states of consciousness and insight.

Moreover, breathwork can also serve as a powerful tool for releasing emotional blockages and promoting psychological healing. Through intentional breathing techniques, individuals can access and release stored emotions and tensions in the body, enabling them to process unresolved trauma and negative patterns more effectively. This process of emotional release and catharsis can be incredibly liberating and transformative, allowing individuals to experience a sense of inner freedom and emotional resilience. By incorporating breathwork into their meditation practice, individuals can create a safe and supportive space for emotional healing and self-exploration, ultimately leading to greater emotional well-being and self-acceptance. Through conscious and mindful breathing, individuals can regulate their nervous system, integrate their mind and body, and access deeper levels of consciousness and emotional healing. Therefore, incorporating breathwork into one's meditation practice can greatly enhance its transformative potential and foster a greater sense of well-being and inner peace.

- Various breathing techniques for relaxation and stress relief

In today's fast-paced world, stress has become a common phenomenon that affects many people. Stress can manifest in various ways, such as feeling anxious, irritable, or overwhelmed. It can also lead to physical symptoms like tension headaches, muscle aches, and digestive issues. In order to manage stress effectively, it is important to find ways to relax and unwind. One effective way to do this is through various breathing techniques that can help calm the mind and body, promoting relaxation and reducing stress levels.

One of the most popular breathing techniques for relaxation and stress relief is deep breathing. Deep breathing involves taking slow, deep breaths, filling the lungs with air and exhaling slowly. This type of breathing can help relax the body and mind by activating the body's relaxation response. When we take deep breaths, it stimulates the vagus nerve, which helps to lower heart rate and blood pressure, leading to a sense of calm and relaxation. Deep breathing can be practiced anywhere, at any time, making it a convenient and effective tool for managing stress.

Another effective breathing technique for relaxation and stress relief is diaphragmatic breathing. Diaphragmatic breathing involves using the diaphragm, a muscle located between the chest and abdomen, to breathe deeply and fully. This type of breathing helps to increase oxygen flow to the body, which can reduce stress and promote relaxation. To practice diaphragmatic breathing, lie down on your back or sit comfortably with one hand on your chest and the other on your abdomen. Inhale deeply through your nose, allowing your abdomen to rise as you fill your lungs with air. Exhale slowly through your mouth, allowing your abdomen to fall as you release the air. Repeat this process several times to help calm your mind and body.

Alternate nostril breathing is another effective breathing technique for relaxation and stress relief. This technique involves breathing through one nostril at a time, alternating between the right and left nostrils. Alternate nostril breathing helps to balance the flow of energy in the body, promoting relaxation and reducing stress. To practice alternate nostril breathing, sit comfortably with your spine straight and close your right nostril with your thumb. Inhale through your left nostril, then close your left nostril with your ring finger and exhale through your right nostril. Inhale through your right nostril, then close your right nostril with your thumb and exhale through your left nostril. Repeat this process several times to help calm your mind and body.

Box breathing is another effective breathing technique for relaxation and stress relief. Box breathing involves inhaling, holding the breath, exhaling, and holding the breath again in a four-count pattern. This technique can help to regulate the breath, calm the mind, and reduce stress levels. To practice box breathing, sit comfortably with your spine straight and inhale deeply through your nose for a count of four. Hold your breath for a count of four, then exhale slowly through your mouth for a count of four. Hold your breath again for a count of four before inhaling again. Repeat this pattern several times to help calm your mind and body. Deep breathing, diaphragmatic breathing, alternate nostril breathing, and box breathing are just a few examples of effective techniques that can help calm the mind and body, reduce stress levels, and promote relaxation. These techniques are easy to learn and can be practiced anywhere, making them convenient tools for managing stress in today's fast-paced world. By incorporating these breathing techniques into your daily routine, you can help to improve your overall well-being and find relief from the stresses of everyday life.

- Incorporating breathwork into daily life for increased mindfulness

Incorporating breathwork into daily life can be a powerful tool for increasing mindfulness and overall well-being. Breathwork, also known as controlled breathing or conscious breathing, involves focusing on the breath and using specific techniques to promote relaxation, reduce stress, and enhance awareness of the present moment. By incorporating breathwork into our daily routines, we can cultivate a greater sense of mindfulness, improve our mental clarity and focus, and create a deeper connection to our inner selves.

One of the key benefits of integrating breathwork into daily life is its ability to help us manage stress and anxiety. When we are stressed or anxious, our breathing tends to become shallow and rapid, which can perpetuate feelings of tension and unease. By practicing deep breathing exercises regularly, we can train our bodies to breathe more deeply and consciously, which in turn can calm the nervous system, reduce stress hormones, and promote a sense of relaxation and well-being. This can be particularly helpful in high-stress situations, such as during exams, presentations, or difficult conversations, where taking a moment to focus on our breath can help us stay calm and centered.

In addition to managing stress, breathwork can also enhance our ability to be present and mindful in our daily lives. Mindfulness is the practice of paying attention to the present moment with openness, curiosity, and acceptance, and breathwork can serve as a powerful anchor for cultivating this state of awareness. By focusing on our breath, we can ground ourselves in the here and now, quiet the chatter of our minds, and tune into the sensations of our bodies. This can help us become more attuned to our thoughts, emotions, and physical sensations, and cultivate a greater sense of self-awareness and presence in each moment.

Furthermore, incorporating breathwork into daily life can also improve our mental clarity and focus. The act of consciously controlling our breath can help us regulate our energy levels, increase oxygen flow to the brain, and enhance cognitive function. By practicing breathwork regularly, we can sharpen our ability to concentrate, make clear decisions, and solve problems more effectively. This can be particularly beneficial for students studying for exams, professionals navigating complex tasks, or anyone seeking to enhance their mental performance in daily life.

Perhaps most importantly, integrating breathwork into our daily routines can help us create a deeper connection to our inner selves and cultivate a greater sense of inner peace and balance. By taking the time to pause and focus on our breath, we can tap into our inner reservoir of strength, wisdom, and intuition. This can help us navigate life's challenges with more resilience, compassion, and grace, and foster a sense of alignment and harmony within ourselves. In a world that is often fast-paced and chaotic, breathwork offers us a powerful tool for grounding ourselves, finding stillness amidst the chaos, and reconnecting with our true essence. By integrating breathwork into our daily routines, we can manage stress and anxiety, cultivate mindfulness and presence, improve mental clarity and focus, and cultivate a greater sense of inner peace and balance. Whether practiced for a few minutes each day or woven into our daily activities, breathwork offers us a simple yet profound way to access the wisdom and vitality that resides within us. So why not take a deep breath, exhale slowly, and begin your journey into the transformative power of breathwork today.

Chapter 11: Meditation for Sleep

- TECHNIQUES FOR USING meditation to improve sleep quality

Sleep is a vital component of overall health and well-being, yet many individuals struggle to achieve quality rest on a consistent basis. Insomnia, restlessness, and other sleep disorders can have a significant impact on one's physical, mental, and emotional health. Fortunately, there are several techniques that can be utilized to improve sleep quality, with meditation being one of the most effective and accessible methods.

Meditation is a practice that involves focusing the mind and cultivating a sense of mindfulness and relaxation. By training the mind to be present and calm, individuals can reduce stress and anxiety, both of which are common culprits of disrupted sleep. Through regular meditation practice, individuals can learn to quiet the mind and let go of racing thoughts, allowing them to enter a state of deep relaxation conducive to a restful night's sleep.

One of the key benefits of using meditation to improve sleep quality is its ability to reduce stress and promote relaxation. Stress and anxiety are major contributors to sleep disturbances, as they can keep the mind in a state of hyperarousal that makes it difficult to fall asleep and stay asleep. By practicing meditation regularly, individuals can learn to manage stress more effectively and cultivate a sense of inner peace and calm that can carry over into their sleep patterns. Meditation helps to activate the body's relaxation response, which can counteract the effects of the stress response and promote a state of physical and mental calmness that is conducive to sleep.

In addition to reducing stress, meditation can also help individuals to regulate their emotions and mood, which can have a significant impact on sleep quality. Negative emotions such as anger, sadness, and frustration can disrupt sleep and lead to insomnia and other sleep disorders. By practicing mindfulness and meditation, individuals can learn to observe their thoughts and feelings without judgment and cultivate a sense of emotional balance and resilience. This can help individuals to let go of negative emotions and promote a more positive and relaxed state of mind that is conducive to sleep.

Another benefit of using meditation to improve sleep quality is its ability to enhance the body's natural sleep-wake cycle. Our bodies have an internal clock known as the circadian rhythm, which regulates the timing of sleep and wakefulness based on external cues such as light and darkness. Disruptions to this rhythm can lead to sleep disturbances and disorders such as insomnia. By practicing meditation regularly, individuals can help to regulate their circadian rhythm and promote a more consistent sleep-wake cycle. Meditation helps to reset the body's internal clock and synchronize it with external cues, which can help individuals to fall asleep more easily and wake up feeling more refreshed and energized.

There are several techniques that can be used to incorporate meditation into a bedtime routine to improve sleep quality. One of the most effective techniques is mindful meditation, which involves focusing on the breath and observing thoughts and sensations without judgment. To practice mindful meditation before bed, individuals can find a comfortable position and close their eyes, then focus on their breath as it enters and leaves the body. If thoughts or distractions arise, individuals can gently redirect their attention back to the breath without getting caught up in them. This practice can help to calm the mind and promote relaxation, making it easier to fall asleep and stay asleep throughout the night.

In addition to mindful meditation, individuals can also utilize guided meditation techniques to improve sleep quality. Guided meditation involves listening to a recorded meditation script or audio track that guides individuals through a series of relaxation exercises and visualizations. These exercises can help to relax the body and mind, promote deep breathing, and cultivate a sense of inner peace and calm that is conducive to sleep. By following along with a guided meditation before bed, individuals can create a soothing and tranquil environment that can help them drift off to sleep more easily and experience a more restful night's sleep. By incorporating meditation into a bedtime routine, individuals can create a calm and peaceful environment that is conducive to restful sleep. Whether through mindful meditation, guided meditation, or other relaxation techniques, meditation can help individuals to quiet the mind, relax the body, and achieve a more restful night's sleep. By practicing meditation regularly and making it a priority in their daily routine, individuals can experience the benefits of improved sleep quality and wake up feeling more refreshed, rejuvenated, and ready to take on the day.

- Creating a bedtime meditation routine

Creating a bedtime meditation routine can be a valuable practice for promoting relaxation, reducing stress, and improving overall sleep quality. By incorporating mindfulness meditation techniques into your nightly routine, you can create a sense of calm and tranquility that can help prepare your mind and body for restful sleep. In this article, we will explore the benefits of bedtime meditation, provide tips for creating a meditation routine, and offer guidance on how to stay consistent with your practice.

One of the key benefits of bedtime meditation is its ability to help calm the mind and reduce stress. In today's fast-paced world, many of us experience high levels of stress throughout the day, which can make it difficult to unwind and relax in the evening. By incorporating meditation into your bedtime routine, you can create a space for yourself to let go of the stresses of the day and focus on the present moment. This can help to quiet the mind, reduce anxiety, and promote a sense of inner peace that can help you drift off to sleep more easily.

Another benefit of bedtime meditation is its ability to help improve sleep quality. Research has shown that regular meditation practice can help regulate the body's stress response system, leading to improved sleep patterns and deeper, more restful sleep. By practicing meditation before bed, you can train your mind and body to relax and unwind, making it easier to fall asleep and stay asleep throughout the night. Additionally, meditation can help reduce the frequency and intensity of intrusive thoughts that can disrupt sleep, allowing you to enjoy a more peaceful and uninterrupted night's rest.

Creating a bedtime meditation routine can be a simple and straightforward process. To begin, find a quiet and comfortable space where you can sit or lie down without distraction. Choose a time that works best for you, whether it's right before bed or earlier in the evening to help wind down. Settle into a comfortable position and close your eyes, taking a few deep breaths to center yourself and bring your awareness to the present moment. Begin by focusing on your breath, noticing the inhale and exhale as it flows in and out of your body. If your mind starts to wander, gently guide your attention back to your breath without judgment.

As you continue to focus on your breath, you may start to notice thoughts and sensations arising in your mind. Instead of trying to push them away, simply observe them with curiosity and let them pass without getting caught up in them. This practice of non-judgmental awareness can help cultivate a sense of mindfulness and inner peace that can carry over into your sleep. If you find it challenging to quiet your mind, you can try using guided meditation recordings or apps to provide structure and support for your practice.

Consistency is key when it comes to developing a bedtime meditation routine. Just like any other habit, it takes time and dedication to establish a regular meditation practice. Start by committing to meditating for a few minutes each night and gradually increasing the duration as you become more comfortable with the practice. Set a specific time each evening to meditate, whether it's right before bed or during a quiet moment earlier in the evening. By creating a routine and sticking to it, you can develop a sense of discipline and commitment that will help you maintain your practice over the long term.

In addition to practicing meditation before bed, you can also incorporate other relaxation techniques into your bedtime routine to further promote restful sleep. This may include gentle stretching exercises, reading a book, taking a warm bath, or listening to calming music. By creating a relaxing and consistent routine, you can signal to your body that it's time to unwind and prepare for sleep. Over time, these practices can help create a sense of ritual and familiarity that can help you transition more easily into a restful and rejuvenating night's sleep.

- Benefits of restful sleep for reducing stress and anxiety

Sleep is a fundamental biological process that is essential for overall health and well-being. Adequate restful sleep is critical for reducing stress and anxiety, as it plays a crucial role in regulating emotions and cognitive function. When we do not get enough sleep or experience poor-quality sleep, our bodies and minds can become overwhelmed, leading to increased levels of stress and anxiety. In this article, we will explore the benefits of restful sleep for reducing stress and anxiety, and discuss some practical strategies for improving sleep quality.

One of the key ways in which restful sleep helps to reduce stress and anxiety is by allowing the body to rest and recharge. During sleep, the body undergoes a variety of important processes, including tissue repair, muscle growth, and the release of hormones that regulate mood and stress levels. When we do not get enough sleep, these processes can be disrupted, leading to increased levels of stress and anxiety. By ensuring that we get an adequate amount of restful sleep each night, we can give our bodies the opportunity to recover and reset, which can help to reduce the impact of stress and anxiety on our overall well-being.

In addition to allowing the body to rest and recharge, restful sleep also plays a critical role in regulating emotions and cognitive function. When we are sleep deprived, our ability to regulate our emotions and respond to stressful situations is significantly impaired. This can lead to increased levels of irritability, anxiety, and difficulty coping with everyday challenges. On the other hand, when we are well-rested, our brains are better able to regulate emotions and make rational decisions, which can help to reduce stress and anxiety. By prioritizing restful sleep, we can better equip ourselves to manage stress and anxiety in a healthy and constructive way.

Furthermore, restful sleep is essential for maintaining a healthy balance of neurotransmitters in the brain, which play a key role in regulating mood and stress levels. When we do not get enough sleep, the balance of neurotransmitters in the brain can be disrupted, leading to increased levels of stress and anxiety. By prioritizing restful sleep, we can help to ensure that our brains have the necessary resources to maintain a healthy balance of neurotransmitters, which can help to reduce the impact of stress and anxiety on our mental health.

It is also worth noting that poor-quality sleep can have a negative impact on our physical health, which can in turn exacerbate stress and anxiety. When we do not get enough restful sleep, our immune system can become compromised, making us more susceptible to illness and infection. This can lead to increased levels of stress and anxiety, as we struggle to cope with the physical symptoms of poor health. By prioritizing restful sleep, we can help to support our immune system and maintain our physical health, which can help to reduce the impact of stress and anxiety on our overall well-being. By prioritizing restful sleep and adopting healthy sleep habits, we can give our bodies and minds the opportunity to rest, recharge, and recover, which can help to reduce the impact of stress and anxiety on our overall well-being. It is important to recognize the importance of restful sleep and to make it a priority in our daily lives, in order to promote optimal health and well-being. By taking steps to improve our sleep quality, we can better equip ourselves to cope with the challenges of everyday life and maintain a healthy balance of stress and anxiety.

Chapter 12: Cultivating Gratitude

- IMPORTANCE OF GRATITUDE in finding inner calm

Gratitude is a powerful tool that can help individuals find inner calm and peace in their lives. It is the practice of acknowledging and appreciating the good things in one's life, both big and small. When we take the time to focus on what we are grateful for, we shift our perspective from what we lack to what we have. This shift in mindset can have profound effects on our overall well-being and can lead to a greater sense of inner calm.

Research has shown that cultivating gratitude can have numerous benefits for mental health and overall happiness. When we express gratitude, our brains release dopamine and serotonin, which are neurotransmitters associated with feelings of happiness and contentment. By focusing on the positive aspects of our lives, we can train our brains to be more resilient and optimistic, even in the face of challenges and setbacks. This can help us navigate difficult times with grace and perspective, leading to a greater sense of inner peace and calm.

Gratitude also has the power to improve relationships and strengthen social connections. When we express gratitude towards others, it can deepen our bonds and create a sense of reciprocity and trust. Gratitude can also help us see the good in people, even when they may have hurt or disappointed us. By practicing gratitude in our relationships, we can foster a greater sense of understanding and empathy, leading to more harmonious and fulfilling connections with others.

In addition to its mental and emotional benefits, gratitude can also have a positive impact on physical health. Studies have shown that grateful individuals have lower levels of stress and inflammation, which are both linked to a range of chronic health conditions. By practicing gratitude regularly, we can reduce the harmful effects of stress on our bodies and improve our overall well-being. This can lead to a greater sense of calm and relaxation, as our bodies are better equipped to cope with the challenges of everyday life.

One of the key aspects of gratitude is mindfulness, the practice of being fully present and aware of our thoughts and feelings without judgment. When we cultivate gratitude, we are more likely to be present in the moment and appreciate the beauty and goodness that surrounds us. This can help us let go of worries about the future or regrets about the past, allowing us to find peace and tranquility in the present moment. By being mindful and grateful, we can cultivate a sense of inner calm that can sustain us through life's ups and downs.

It is important to note that gratitude is a skill that can be cultivated and developed over time. Like any practice, it requires dedication and effort to become a natural part of our daily lives. One way to incorporate gratitude into your routine is to keep a gratitude journal, where you can write down three things you are grateful for each day. This simple exercise can help you shift your focus from what is lacking in your life to what is abundant and meaningful. Over time, you may find that practicing gratitude becomes second nature, leading to a greater sense of inner calm and peace. By focusing on the positive aspects of our lives and expressing appreciation for the good things we have, we can cultivate a greater sense of happiness, resilience, and well-being. Gratitude has the power to improve our mental, emotional, and physical health, as well as strengthen our relationships and deepen our connections with others. By practicing gratitude regularly and mindfully, we can create a foundation of inner calm that can sustain us through life's challenges and uncertainties.

- How gratitude practices reduce stress and anxiety

Gratitude practices have been increasingly recognized as powerful tools for reducing stress and anxiety in individuals. In recent years, there has been a growing body of research that highlights the benefits of incorporating gratitude into one's daily routine. By fostering a sense of appreciation and thankfulness, gratitude practices have been shown to improve mental well-being and overall quality of life. This article will delve into the ways in which gratitude practices can help alleviate stress and anxiety, as well as provide practical tips for incorporating gratitude into your daily life.

Stress and anxiety are common mental health issues that can have a significant impact on an individual's well-being. The fast-paced nature of modern life, combined with constant exposure to stressors, has led to an increase in stress-related disorders. Research has shown that chronic stress can have detrimental effects on both physical and mental health, leading to an array of health problems such as high blood pressure, heart disease, and depression. Similarly, anxiety disorders can interfere with daily life, making it difficult for individuals to function effectively in their personal and professional lives.

Gratitude practices offer a unique solution to combatting stress and anxiety, as they focus on shifting one's perspective from focusing on what is lacking in life to appreciating what one already has. By cultivating a sense of gratitude, individuals can reframe their thoughts and emotions, leading to a more positive outlook on life. Gratitude has been described as a state of mind that involves acknowledging and appreciating the good things in one's life, no matter how small they may seem. This shift in perspective can have profound effects on one's mental health, helping to reduce stress and anxiety levels.

One way in which gratitude practices can reduce stress and anxiety is by promoting positive emotions and feelings of well-being. When individuals focus on the things they are thankful for, they are able to experience a sense of joy and contentment. This positive emotion can act as a buffer against stress, helping individuals to cope with life's challenges more effectively. Research has shown that practicing gratitude can increase levels of dopamine and serotonin in the brain, leading to an overall improvement in mood and emotional well-being. By cultivating positive emotions through gratitude practices, individuals can reduce feelings of anxiety and stress.

In addition to promoting positive emotions, gratitude practices can also help individuals develop a sense of resilience in the face of adversity. When individuals practice gratitude regularly, they are more likely to adopt a mindset of abundance and abundance, rather than scarcity. This shift in mindset can help individuals to cope with stress and anxiety more effectively, as they are able to see challenges as opportunities for growth and development. By focusing on the things they are grateful for, individuals can build resilience and strength, enabling them to navigate through life's ups and downs with greater ease.

Moreover, gratitude practices can help individuals to cultivate a sense of mindfulness and presence in their daily lives. Mindfulness involves being fully present in the moment, without judgment or attachment to past or future events. By practicing gratitude, individuals can train their minds to focus on the present moment and appreciate the beauty and wonder of life. This can help individuals to reduce stress and anxiety, as they are able to let go of worries and concerns about the future and instead focus on the here and now. By cultivating mindfulness through gratitude practices, individuals can experience a greater sense of peace, calm, and clarity in their daily lives.

Practical ways to incorporate gratitude into one's daily routine include keeping a gratitude journal, practicing mindfulness meditation, and expressing gratitude to others. Keeping a gratitude journal involves writing down three things you are thankful for each day, whether big or small. This simple practice can help individuals to cultivate a sense of appreciation and thankfulness, leading to a more positive outlook on life. Similarly, practicing mindfulness meditation can help individuals to develop a greater sense of presence and awareness, enabling them to fully experience and appreciate the present moment. To culminate, expressing gratitude to others can help individuals to strengthen their social connections and foster a sense of community and belonging. By expressing appreciation and gratitude to friends, family, and colleagues, individuals can build positive relationships and support networks that can help them cope with stress and anxiety more effectively. By fostering a sense of appreciation and thankfulness, individuals can cultivate positive emotions, resilience, mindfulness, and social connections. By incorporating gratitude into their daily routine, individuals can experience a greater sense of well-being and quality of life. So why not start practicing gratitude today and reap the many benefits it has to offer.

- Techniques for developing a gratitude mindset through meditation

Gratitude is an essential component of well-being and personal growth. Adopting a mindset of gratitude can lead to increased positive emotions, improved relationships, and overall life satisfaction. One powerful tool for cultivating gratitude is meditation. Through the practice of meditation, individuals can train their minds to focus on the present moment and appreciate the blessings in their lives.

One technique for developing a gratitude mindset through meditation is mindfulness meditation. In mindfulness meditation, individuals are encouraged to pay attention to their thoughts and feelings without judgment. By observing their thoughts in a non-reactive way, individuals can become more aware of the things in their lives that they are grateful for. Practicing mindfulness meditation can help individuals shift their focus from what they lack to what they have, fostering a sense of gratitude and contentment.

Another technique for developing a gratitude mindset through meditation is loving-kindness meditation. In loving-kindness meditation, individuals cultivate feelings of compassion and goodwill towards themselves and others. By sending positive thoughts and well-wishes to yourself and those around you, you can generate feelings of gratitude and appreciation. This practice can help individuals develop a more positive outlook on life and deepen their sense of connection with others.

Visualization meditation is another powerful technique for developing a gratitude mindset. In visualization meditation, individuals are encouraged to imagine themselves in a peaceful and serene environment, surrounded by the things they are grateful for. By vividly picturing the things that bring them joy and fulfillment, individuals can cultivate feelings of gratitude and appreciation. Visualization meditation can help individuals reframe their perspective on life and focus on the positive aspects of their experiences.

Gratitude journaling is a complementary practice that can enhance the benefits of meditation in developing a gratitude mindset. By writing down the things you are grateful for each day, you can reinforce your feelings of gratitude and cultivate a mindset of appreciation. Keeping a gratitude journal can help individuals reflect on the positive aspects of their lives and maintain a sense of gratitude even in challenging times. Combining gratitude journaling with meditation can amplify the effects of both practices and help individuals develop a deeper sense of gratitude. By incorporating mindfulness meditation, loving-kindness meditation, visualization meditation, and gratitude journaling into your daily routine, you can train your mind to focus on the blessings in your life and appreciate the richness of your experiences. With consistent practice and dedication, you can develop a deeper sense of gratitude that will enrich your life and enhance your overall happiness and fulfillment.

Chapter 13: Overcoming Negative Thoughts

- STRATEGIES FOR MANAGING negative thought patterns

It is important to recognize when these negative thoughts arise and to have strategies in place for managing them effectively. In this article, we will explore some of the key strategies for managing negative thought patterns and how they can help us lead a more positive and fulfilling life.

One of the first steps in managing negative thought patterns is to become aware of when they occur. This can be challenging, as negative thoughts often occur automatically and without conscious awareness. However, by taking the time to notice when these thoughts are present, we can begin to identify patterns and triggers that may be contributing to them. Keeping a journal can be a helpful tool in this process, as it allows us to track our thoughts and feelings over time and identify any recurring themes.

Once we have become more aware of our negative thought patterns, we can begin to challenge and reframe them. This involves questioning the validity of these thoughts and looking for evidence to support or refute them. For example, if we find ourselves thinking "I'm a failure" after making a mistake at work, we can ask ourselves if this thought is truly accurate or if there are other ways to interpret the situation. By challenging our negative thoughts in this way, we can begin to shift our perspective and develop a more balanced and realistic view of ourselves and our circumstances.

In addition to challenging negative thoughts, it can also be helpful to practice self-compassion and kindness towards ourselves. Negative thought patterns often involve harsh self-criticism and judgment, which can be damaging to our self-esteem and well-being. By cultivating a sense of self-compassion, we can learn to treat ourselves with the same kindness and understanding that we would offer to a friend in a similar situation. This can help us to break free from the cycle of negative thinking and develop a more positive and nurturing relationship with ourselves.

Another effective strategy for managing negative thought patterns is mindfulness meditation. Mindfulness involves paying attention to the present moment without judgment, allowing us to observe our thoughts and feelings without getting caught up in them. By practicing mindfulness regularly, we can learn to recognize when negative thoughts arise and let them pass without becoming attached to them. This can help us to develop a greater sense of inner peace and resilience in the face of challenging situations.

In addition to these strategies, seeking support from a therapist or counselor can be beneficial for managing negative thought patterns. A trained professional can help us explore the root causes of our negative thinking and develop personalized strategies for overcoming them. Therapy can provide a safe and supportive space for us to work through our thoughts and feelings, helping us to gain insight into our patterns and develop healthier ways of coping. By recognizing when negative thoughts arise, challenging them, and practicing mindfulness and self-compassion, we can begin to break free from the cycle of negative thinking and lead a more positive and fulfilling life. Seeking support from a therapist can also be helpful in this process, providing us with guidance and tools for overcoming our negative thought patterns and building a more resilient and positive mindset. With dedication and perseverance, it is possible to overcome negative thought patterns and cultivate a greater sense of well-being and happiness in our lives.

- Using meditation to reframe negative thoughts

Meditation is a powerful tool that can be used to cultivate a more positive mindset and reframe negative thoughts. When we engage in meditation practices, we are able to quiet the mind and create space for self-reflection and introspection. Through the practice of meditation, we can learn to observe our thoughts without judgment and begin to cultivate a greater sense of self-awareness.

One of the key benefits of meditation is its ability to help us become more aware of our thought patterns. Many of us have a tendency to dwell on negative thoughts and allow them to spiral out of control. Through meditation, we can learn to recognize when negative thoughts arise and gently guide our minds back to a more positive focus. By cultivating this awareness, we can begin to break free from the cycle of negative thinking and cultivate a more positive mindset.

In addition to increasing self-awareness, meditation also helps to calm the nervous system and reduce stress. When we are in a state of stress, our bodies produce cortisol, a hormone that can have negative effects on both our physical and mental health. By engaging in regular meditation practices, we can reduce the levels of cortisol in our bodies and create a greater sense of calm and relaxation.

Furthermore, meditation has been shown to improve overall mental health and well-being. Research has shown that regular meditation can help to reduce symptoms of anxiety and depression, as well as improve overall mood and emotional stability. By reframing negative thoughts through the practice of meditation, we can create a more positive outlook on life and improve our overall mental health.

It is important to note that meditation is not a quick fix for negative thinking; it is a practice that requires dedication and commitment. Like any skill, the more we practice meditation, the more we will benefit from its effects. It is important to approach meditation with an open mind and a willingness to explore new ways of thinking.

There are many different types of meditation practices that can be used to reframe negative thoughts. Some individuals may find that mindfulness meditation, which involves focusing on the present moment without judgment, is particularly helpful in cultivating a more positive mindset. Others may find that loving-kindness meditation, which involves sending compassion and love to oneself and others, is more effective in reframing negative thoughts.

It is also important to remember that meditation is not a one-size-fits-all practice. What works for one person may not work for another. It is important to explore different meditation practices and find the one that resonates most with you. Additionally, it is important to practice meditation regularly in order to see the benefits over time. Through the practice of meditation, we can increase self-awareness, reduce stress, improve overall mental health, and create a greater sense of calm and relaxation. By approaching meditation with an open mind and a willingness to explore new ways of thinking, we can begin to reap the many benefits that meditation has to offer.

- Cultivating a positive and resilient mindset through mindfulness

Cultivating a positive and resilient mindset through mindfulness is a practice that has gained significant attention in recent years, as individuals seek ways to cope with the challenges and uncertainties of daily life. Mindfulness, often defined as the ability to be fully present in the moment without judgment, has been shown to have a variety of benefits for mental health and overall well-being. By consciously focusing on the present moment and being aware of one's thoughts and emotions, individuals can develop a greater sense of self-awareness, emotional regulation, and resilience in the face of adversity.

One of the key components of cultivating a positive and resilient mindset through mindfulness is developing a daily practice of mindfulness meditation. This practice involves setting aside time each day to sit quietly and focus on the breath, bodily sensations, or the present moment. Through regular practice, individuals can train their minds to be more attuned to the present moment, cultivating a sense of calm and clarity that can help them navigate challenging situations with greater ease. Research has shown that mindfulness meditation can have a variety of benefits for mental health, including reducing stress, anxiety, and depression, while also improving attention, memory, and decision-making skills.

In addition to mindfulness meditation, another important aspect of cultivating a positive and resilient mindset is learning to practice mindfulness in daily life. This involves bringing a sense of awareness and presence to everyday activities, such as eating, walking, or engaging in conversations. By paying attention to the present moment and being fully engaged in whatever task is at hand, individuals can develop a greater sense of appreciation for the simple joys of life and reduce the tendency to dwell on past regrets or future anxieties. This practice of mindfulness in daily life can help individuals build resilience by enabling them to respond more skillfully to stressors and challenges as they arise.

Another key aspect of cultivating a positive and resilient mindset through mindfulness is cultivating self-compassion and self-acceptance. Mindfulness involves approaching one's thoughts, emotions, and experiences with an attitude of non-judgment and curiosity, rather than criticism or avoidance. By practicing self-compassion, individuals can learn to treat themselves with kindness and understanding, particularly in times of difficulty or suffering. Research has shown that self-compassion is associated with greater emotional resilience, lower levels of anxiety and depression, and higher levels of overall well-being.

Furthermore, developing a positive and resilient mindset through mindfulness involves cultivating a sense of gratitude and appreciation for the present moment. By focusing on the positive aspects of one's life and acknowledging the blessings and opportunities that exist, individuals can shift their perspective from one of lack and scarcity to one of abundance and gratitude. Research has shown that gratitude is associated with greater levels of happiness, resilience, and overall well-being, as individuals learn to focus on what they have rather than what they lack. By developing a daily practice of mindfulness meditation, learning to practice mindfulness in daily life, cultivating self-compassion and self-acceptance, and fostering gratitude and appreciation, individuals can build resilience and improve their ability to cope with the challenges and uncertainties of life. Through mindfulness, individuals can develop a greater sense of self-awareness, emotional regulation, and resilience, enabling them to navigate life's ups and downs with grace and ease.

Chapter 14: Self-Compassion Meditation

- UNDERSTANDING SELF-compassion and its impact on mental health

Self-compassion is a concept that has gained increasing attention in the fields of psychology and mental health in recent years. Defined as the ability to treat oneself with kindness and understanding in times of struggle or failure, self-compassion has been linked to a wide range of positive mental health outcomes. In this essay, we will explore the concept of self-compassion in detail, examining its components, the benefits it offers, and its impact on mental health.

Self-compassion is often described as having three main components: self-kindness, common humanity, and mindfulness. Self-kindness involves treating oneself with the same warmth and understanding that one would offer to a friend in times of difficulty. This means being gentle with oneself, rather than harshly self-critical. Common humanity is the recognition that suffering and imperfection are universal human experiences, and that one is not alone in experiencing challenges and setbacks. Lastly, mindfulness involves being present and aware of one's thoughts and feelings in a non-judgmental way, rather than being consumed by self-criticism or negative self-talk.

Research has shown that self-compassion is associated with a wide range of mental health benefits. People who are more self-compassionate tend to have higher levels of self-esteem, lower levels of anxiety and depression, and better overall psychological well-being. They also tend to have healthier coping strategies for dealing with stressful situations, such as seeking social support and engaging in self-care activities. Self-compassion has also been linked to greater resilience in the face of adversity, as individuals who are able to offer themselves kindness and understanding are better able to bounce back from setbacks and continue to pursue their goals.

One of the key ways in which self-compassion benefits mental health is by promoting a sense of emotional regulation and self-soothing. When we are able to offer ourselves kindness and understanding in times of distress, we are more likely to be able to regulate our emotions and prevent ourselves from becoming overwhelmed by negative thoughts and feelings. This can help us to avoid spiraling into a cycle of self-criticism and rumination, which can be damaging to our mental health. By practicing self-compassion, we can learn to soothe ourselves in moments of difficulty and cultivate a more positive and nurturing internal dialogue.

Furthermore, self-compassion has been shown to be particularly beneficial for individuals who struggle with conditions such as anxiety and depression. People with these conditions often experience high levels of self-criticism and self-judgment, which can exacerbate their symptoms and interfere with their ability to cope effectively. By cultivating self-compassion, individuals can break this cycle of negativity and begin to treat themselves with the kindness and understanding they deserve. This can lead to a reduction in symptoms of anxiety and depression, as well as an improvement in overall mental well-being.

It is important to note that self-compassion is a skill that can be developed and cultivated over time through practice and self-awareness. Just as we can learn to be more compassionate and understanding towards others, we can also learn to extend the same kindness and understanding to ourselves. This may involve challenging ingrained beliefs and habits of self-criticism, as well as practicing self-kindness and self-care on a regular basis. By making a conscious effort to be more self-compassionate, we can begin to transform our relationship with ourselves and pave the way for improved mental health and well-being. By treating ourselves with kindness and understanding, we can cultivate a more positive internal dialogue, reduce symptoms of anxiety and depression, and build resilience in the face of adversity. Developing self-compassion is a skill that requires practice and self-awareness, but the benefits it offers are well worth the effort. By learning to be more self-compassionate, we can create a foundation of self-love and self-acceptance that can help us navigate life's challenges with grace and resilience.

- Techniques for practicing self-compassion meditation

Self-compassion meditation is a powerful tool that can help individuals cultivate a sense of kindness and understanding towards themselves. In today's fast-paced and often stressful world, it is easy to be overly critical of oneself and to engage in negative self-talk. Self-compassion meditation offers a way to counteract these harmful tendencies and promote self-acceptance and self-love. By practicing self-compassion meditation regularly, individuals can learn to treat themselves with the same kindness and care that they would offer to a friend in need.

There are several techniques that can be employed when practicing self-compassion meditation. One common approach is to begin by finding a quiet and comfortable space where you can relax and focus on your breathing. Take a few deep breaths, allowing yourself to settle into a calm and centered state. Once you feel grounded, begin to repeat a series of self-compassionate affirmations or mantras. These may include statements such as "I am worthy of love and kindness," "I forgive myself for any mistakes I have made," or "I am deserving of compassion and understanding." Repeat these affirmations slowly and gently, allowing yourself to truly absorb their meaning and intention.

Another technique that can be helpful in self-compassion meditation is guided visualization. This involves imagining yourself in a peaceful and nurturing environment, such as a beautiful garden or a cozy room. As you visualize this scene, focus on cultivating feelings of warmth, love, and acceptance towards yourself. Imagine wrapping yourself in a cocoon of compassion and letting go of any negative thoughts or judgments. Allow yourself to bask in the glow of this self-compassionate energy, knowing that you are deserving of all the kindness and care that you can offer.

Body scan meditation is another technique that can be beneficial when practicing self-compassion meditation. This involves systematically scanning your body for any areas of tension or discomfort and then sending love and healing energy to those areas. Begin by focusing on your feet and working your way up to your head, paying attention to any sensations you may be experiencing. As you encounter areas of tension or pain, breathe deeply into them and imagine sending waves of compassion and kindness to those areas.

Allow yourself to release any negative energy and replace it with feelings of love and acceptance.

One of the key components of self-compassion meditation is cultivating a sense of mindfulness. This involves being fully present in the moment and observing your thoughts and feelings without judgment. When practicing self-compassion meditation, it is important to approach yourself with curiosity and openness, rather than criticism or harshness. By acknowledging and accepting your thoughts and emotions as they arise, you can begin to cultivate a greater sense of self-awareness and self-compassion. Remember that it is perfectly normal to experience a range of emotions during meditation, and that the goal is not to suppress these feelings but to observe them with compassion and understanding.

In addition to these techniques, there are a few other strategies that can help enhance your self-compassion meditation practice. One important tip is to set aside a dedicated time each day for meditation, ideally in the morning or evening when you are least likely to be interrupted. Consistency is key when it comes to cultivating self-compassion, so make a commitment to yourself to practice regularly. You may also find it helpful to keep a journal of your meditation experiences, noting any insights or breakthroughs that arise during your practice. This can help you track your progress and identify any patterns or obstacles that may be holding you back.

Ultimately, the goal of self-compassion meditation is to foster a sense of kindness, acceptance, and understanding towards oneself. By practicing these techniques regularly, individuals can learn to quiet their inner critic and embrace themselves with open arms. Remember that self-compassion is not a destination, but a journey, and that it is okay to stumble along the way. Be patient and gentle with yourself as you explore the practice of self-compassion meditation, and know that each moment of self-reflection and self-love brings you closer to a place of peace and wholeness.

- Benefits of self-compassion for reducing self-criticism and anxiety

Self-compassion is a concept that has gained momentum in recent years as a powerful tool for reducing self-criticism and anxiety. Self-compassion involves treating oneself with the same kindness and understanding that one would offer to a friend in times of struggle or distress. It encompasses three key components: self-kindness, common humanity, and mindfulness.

The first component of self-compassion is self-kindness, which involves being gentle and understanding towards oneself rather than harshly self-critical. Many individuals have a tendency to be overly critical of themselves, holding themselves to impossibly high standards and berating themselves when they fall short. This constant self-criticism can be damaging to one's mental and emotional well-being, contributing to feelings of worthlessness and inadequacy. By practicing self-kindness, individuals can learn to treat themselves with compassion and understanding, fostering a more positive and nurturing relationship with themselves.

The second component of self-compassion is common humanity, which involves recognizing that suffering and imperfection are part of the human experience. When individuals feel overwhelmed by self-criticism and anxiety, they may believe that they are alone in their struggles and that there is something inherently wrong with them. This can lead to feelings of isolation and shame, further exacerbating their distress. By acknowledging that everyone experiences difficulties and imperfections, individuals can develop a sense of connection and belonging, reducing feelings of isolation and self-judgment.

The third component of self-compassion is mindfulness, which involves being present and aware of one's thoughts and feelings without judgment. Mindfulness allows individuals to observe their self-critical thoughts and anxious feelings without becoming overwhelmed by them. By cultivating a nonjudgmental and accepting attitude towards their inner experiences, individuals can develop greater emotional resilience and self-compassion. Mindfulness practices such as meditation and deep breathing can help individuals become more present and attuned to their inner experiences, promoting a sense of calm and self-acceptance.

Research has shown that self-compassion is associated with a wide range of psychological benefits, including reduced levels of self-criticism and anxiety. Studies have found that individuals who practice self-compassion are less likely to engage in negative self-talk and rumination, which are common features of self-criticism. By treating themselves with kindness and understanding, individuals can break the cycle of self-criticism and develop a more compassionate and nurturing relationship with themselves. This can lead to increased feelings of self-worth and self-acceptance, as well as a greater sense of emotional well-being.

In addition to reducing self-criticism, self-compassion has also been shown to be effective in reducing anxiety. When individuals practice self-compassion, they are better able to cope with stressful situations and difficult emotions. By approaching themselves with kindness and mindfulness, individuals can create a sense of safety and security within themselves, reducing feelings of fear and anxiety. Research has found that self-compassion is associated with lower levels of anxiety and higher levels of emotional resilience, allowing individuals to navigate life's challenges with greater ease and confidence. By cultivating self-kindness, common humanity, and mindfulness, individuals can break free from the grip of self-judgment and develop a more compassionate and nurturing relationship with themselves. Through practicing self-compassion, individuals can learn to embrace their imperfections and challenges with grace and understanding, leading to a greater sense of peace and self-acceptance.

Chapter 15: Mindful Eating Meditation

- BENEFITS OF MINDFUL eating for improving digestion and overall well-being

Mindful eating is a practice that involves paying full attention to the experience of eating and drinking, both inside and outside the body. This means being fully present in the moment, focusing on the tastes, smells, textures, and sensations of the food, as well as on the thoughts, feelings, and bodily sensations that arise during the meal. By cultivating mindfulness in this way, one can develop a deeper appreciation and understanding of one's relationship with food, leading to improved digestion and overall well-being.

One of the key benefits of mindful eating is its impact on digestion. Digestion is a complex process that involves multiple organs and systems working together to break down food into nutrients that the body can absorb and use. When we eat mindlessly, we are more likely to overeat, eat too quickly, or eat foods that are not well-suited to our individual needs and preferences. This can lead to indigestion, bloating, gas, and other digestive issues. By contrast, when we eat mindfully, we are more attuned to our body's signals of hunger and fullness, as well as to the quality and quantity of the foods we are consuming. This can help us make better choices about what, when, and how much to eat, leading to improved digestion and gut health.

In addition to benefiting digestion, mindful eating can also have a positive impact on overall well-being. Research has shown that mindfulness practices, such as mindfulness-based eating awareness training (MB-EAT), can help reduce stress, anxiety, and depression, as well as improve mood, self-esteem, and body image. By focusing on the present moment and cultivating a non-judgmental attitude towards our thoughts, emotions, and sensations, we can develop a greater sense of peace, balance, and self-acceptance. This can lead to a more positive relationship with food and with ourselves, promoting greater overall well-being.

Furthermore, mindful eating can also help improve our relationship with food in other ways. Many of us have complex and often fraught relationships with food, stemming from cultural, social, psychological, and environmental factors. We may have learned to use food as a way to cope with stress, boredom, loneliness, or other emotions, leading to patterns of emotional eating, binge eating, or restrictive eating. By practicing mindful eating, we can become more aware of the underlying reasons for our eating habits and develop healthier ways of relating to food and our bodies. This can help us break free from destructive patterns and cultivate a more balanced and intuitive approach to eating.

Moreover, mindful eating can also enhance our enjoyment of food and our overall quality of life. In our fast-paced, busy, and often stressful modern world, it is easy to rush through meals or eat on the go, without truly savoring the experience. By slowing down, tuning in, and savoring each bite, we can fully appreciate the flavors, textures, and aromas of our food, as well as the social and cultural aspects of eating. This can heighten our sensory awareness, gratification, and pleasure, making eating a more meaningful and satisfying experience. In this way, mindful eating can help us cultivate a greater sense of joy, gratitude, and connection in our lives. By bringing greater awareness, presence, and intentionality to our eating habits, we can enhance our digestive health, promote emotional and psychological balance, improve our relationship with food, and increase our enjoyment of meals. Whether you are looking to address digestive issues, reduce stress, enhance self-care, or simply savor the pleasures of eating, incorporating mindfulness into your daily eating routine can have profound and lasting effects on your health and happiness. So why not give it a try and see the positive impact it can have on your digestion and well-being.

- Steps for practicing mindful eating meditation

Mindful eating meditation is a practice that involves bringing awareness and attention to the act of eating. By being fully present in the moment and engaging all of our senses, we can cultivate a deeper connection to our food and our bodies. This practice can help us develop a healthier relationship with food, reduce mindless eating, and increase our overall sense of well-being. In this article, we will explore the steps for practicing mindful eating meditation and how to incorporate this practice into our daily lives.

The first step in practicing mindful eating meditation is to create a peaceful and conducive environment for eating. Find a quiet and comfortable place to sit down and eat without distractions. Turn off the television, put away electronic devices, and focus solely on the act of eating. This will help you to fully immerse yourself in the experience and connect with the food you are consuming.

Next, take a moment to express gratitude for the food in front of you. Before you take your first bite, pause and reflect on the journey that the food has taken to reach your plate. Consider the farmers who grew the ingredients, the workers who harvested and processed the food, and the cooks who prepared the meal. By expressing gratitude, you can cultivate a sense of appreciation for the nourishment that the food provides.

As you begin to eat, pay attention to the appearance, smell, and texture of the food. Notice the colors, shapes, and patterns on your plate. Take a moment to inhale the aroma of the food and savor the scent. Linger over the texture of each bite, noticing how it feels in your mouth and how it changes as you chew. By engaging all of your senses, you can fully experience the pleasure of eating and become more attuned to your body's hunger cues.

While you eat, focus on the sensations in your body. Notice the physical sensations of hunger and fullness, as well as any cravings or aversions that arise. Pay attention to how each bite affects your body and how the food makes you feel. Check in with your body periodically to assess your level of hunger and satisfaction. By tuning into your body's signals, you can eat in a way that honors your hunger and respects your fullness.

It is also important to practice mindful eating by being present and non-judgmental in your experience. Avoid distractions and multi-tasking while eating, such as watching television, working on the computer, or reading a book. Instead, focus on the act of eating and savor each bite without judgment. If your mind wanders or you become distracted, gently bring your attention back to the present moment and the food in front of you. By being fully present, you can cultivate mindfulness and awareness in your eating habits.

Another important aspect of mindful eating meditation is to chew each bite slowly and thoroughly. Take the time to chew your food completely before swallowing, savoring the flavors and textures with each bite. Chewing slowly can improve digestion, reduce bloating, and help you feel more satisfied with your meal. By slowing down the eating process, you can also become more aware of when you are full and prevent overeating.

In addition to chewing slowly, it can also be beneficial to take breaks during your meal to pause and reflect on your experience. Put your utensils down between bites, take a deep breath, and check in with how you are feeling. Notice any emotions or thoughts that arise as you eat and allow yourself to experience them without judgment. Taking breaks can help you to reconnect with your body and mind, and make more conscious choices about what and how you eat.

In closing, after you have finished eating, take a moment to reflect on your experience and express gratitude for the nourishment you have received. Notice any sensations or feelings that arise in your body after the meal, such as satisfaction, fullness, or contentment. Consider how the food has nourished and replenished you, and how you can carry this sense of gratitude and awareness with you throughout the rest of your day. By practicing mindful eating meditation, you can cultivate a deeper connection to your food, your body, and yourself.

- Cultivating awareness and appreciation for food through meditation

Food is an essential part of our daily lives, yet many of us often take it for granted. We rush through meals, eating quickly without truly savoring the flavors and textures of what we are consuming. This lack of awareness and appreciation for food not only deprives us of the pleasure that comes from eating mindfully, but it can also lead to unhealthy eating habits and poor digestion. By cultivating awareness and appreciation for food through meditation, we can transform our relationship with food and create a more mindful approach to eating.

Meditation is a powerful tool for developing mindfulness, which is the practice of being fully present and aware in the moment. When we eat mindfully, we are more attuned to the sensations of eating – the taste, smell, texture, and even the sounds of our food. By bringing our full attention to the act of eating, we can experience a deeper connection to our food and a greater appreciation for the nourishment it provides. Meditation can help us to slow down and fully engage with our meals, allowing us to savor each bite and cultivate a sense of gratitude for the food on our plate.

One of the key aspects of cultivating awareness and appreciation for food through meditation is to approach eating with a sense of intention and presence. Before you begin your meal, take a moment to center yourself and focus on your breathing. Deep, mindful breaths can help you to relax and bring your attention to the present moment. As you sit down to eat, take a few moments to express gratitude for the food in front of you and the people who helped to bring it to your table. This simple act of acknowledgment can help to cultivate a sense of reverence for the nourishment that food provides.

During the meal, pay attention to the sensations of eating – the flavors, textures, and smells of your food. Take your time to chew each bite slowly and mindfully, savoring the experience of eating. Notice how the food feels in your mouth, how it tastes on your tongue, and how it makes you feel as you eat it. By bringing your full attention to the act of eating, you can develop a greater appreciation for the food you are consuming and the nourishment it provides to your body and mind.

Meditation can also help us to become more aware of our body's signals of hunger and fullness, allowing us to eat in a way that is attuned to our body's needs. By tuning into our body's sensations, we can differentiate between true hunger and emotional or boredom eating, and make healthier choices about when and what to eat. When we eat mindfully, we are more in tune with how our body responds to different foods, allowing us to make choices that support our overall health and well-being.

Cultivating awareness and appreciation for food through meditation can also have a positive impact on our mental and emotional well-being. By approaching eating with mindfulness and presence, we can reduce stress and anxiety around food, and develop a more peaceful and balanced relationship with eating. Meditation can help us to release any judgments or negative beliefs we may have about food, allowing us to approach eating with a sense of curiosity and openness. By cultivating a more mindful approach to eating, we can experience greater satisfaction and pleasure in our meals, and create a deeper connection to the nourishment that food provides. By bringing mindfulness and presence to the act of eating, we can experience a deeper connection to our food and develop a greater appreciation for the nourishment it provides. Through meditation, we can become more attuned to our body's signals of hunger and fullness, make healthier choices about when and what to eat, and develop a more peaceful and balanced relationship with food. By incorporating mindfulness into our meals, we can savor the flavors and textures of our food, experience greater satisfaction and pleasure in eating, and create a more mindful approach to nourishing our bodies and minds.

Chapter 16: Finding Balance and Prioritizing Self-Care

- IMPORTANCE OF CREATING balance in life for reducing stress and anxiety

In today's fast-paced and demanding world, stress and anxiety have become increasingly prevalent issues that can have detrimental effects on our mental and physical well-being. The pressure to excel in our careers, maintain fulfilling relationships, and achieve personal goals can often leave us feeling overwhelmed and exhausted. However, creating balance in our lives is essential for reducing stress and anxiety and promoting overall health and happiness.

One of the key benefits of creating balance in life is that it allows us to prioritize our physical and mental well-being. When we are constantly on the go and neglecting our own needs, we are more susceptible to burnout, fatigue, and chronic stress. By taking the time to rest, relax, and engage in self-care activities, we can recharge our batteries and improve our ability to cope with life's challenges. Engaging in activities such as exercise, meditation, and spending time in nature can also help to reduce stress and anxiety by promoting relaxation and a sense of calm.

Another important aspect of creating balance in life is setting boundaries and learning to say no when necessary. Many of us struggle with saying yes to every request or opportunity that comes our way, which can lead to feeling overwhelmed and overextended. By setting limits on our time and energy and prioritizing tasks and commitments, we can avoid spreading ourselves too thin and reduce the risk of burnout. Learning to delegate tasks, ask for help, and prioritize our own needs can help us manage our stress levels and create a more balanced and fulfilling life.

In addition to prioritizing self-care and setting boundaries, creating balance in life also involves fostering meaningful connections and relationships with others. Humans are social beings, and having a support system in place can help to reduce feelings of isolation and loneliness, which are common triggers for stress and anxiety. Cultivating strong relationships with friends, family, and colleagues can provide us with a sense of belonging, support, and comfort during times of stress and uncertainty. Taking the time to nurture these relationships through regular communication, quality time together, and acts of kindness can help us feel more connected and supported, reducing our overall levels of stress and anxiety.

Furthermore, creating balance in life involves finding a sense of purpose and meaning that goes beyond the daily grind of work and responsibilities. Engaging in activities that bring us joy, fulfillment, and a sense of accomplishment can help us feel more satisfied with our lives and reduce feelings of stress and anxiety. Whether it's pursuing a hobby, volunteering for a cause we care about, or setting personal goals and working towards them, finding meaning and purpose in our lives can help us stay motivated and resilient in the face of challenges. By aligning our values and priorities with our actions and choices, we can create a sense of balance and harmony that promotes overall well-being and reduces stress and anxiety. By prioritizing self-care, setting boundaries, fostering meaningful connections, and finding purpose and meaning in our lives, we can create a sense of harmony and fulfillment that helps us navigate life's challenges with resilience and ease. Remember that it's okay to prioritize your own needs and make time for activities that bring you joy and relaxation. By taking care of yourself and creating a balanced and fulfilling life, you can reduce stress and anxiety and live a more peaceful and fulfilling existence.

- Tips for prioritizing self-care and setting boundaries

In today's fast-paced and demanding world, prioritizing self-care and setting boundaries has become more important than ever. Taking care of yourself both physically and mentally is essential for maintaining overall well-being and preventing burnout. Setting boundaries allows you to protect your time, energy, and mental health, and ensures that you are able to focus on what truly matters to you. In this article, we will discuss some tips for prioritizing self-care and setting boundaries in order to create a healthier and more balanced lifestyle.

First and foremost, it is important to recognize the importance of self-care and prioritize it in your daily routine. This can include activities such as exercise, meditation, spending time with loved ones, engaging in hobbies, or simply taking time to relax and unwind. By making self-care a priority, you are investing in your own well-being and ensuring that you have the energy and resilience to handle life's challenges. Setting aside time each day for self-care can help you recharge and rejuvenate, and ultimately lead to a more fulfilling and balanced life.

In addition to prioritizing self-care, setting boundaries is crucial for maintaining healthy relationships and protecting your own well-being. Boundaries are guidelines that you establish for yourself in order to protect your physical, emotional, and mental health. They can help you establish limits with others and prevent you from being taken advantage of or feeling overwhelmed. Setting boundaries can also help you communicate your needs and expectations more effectively, and ensure that you are able to maintain a healthy work-life balance.

One tip for setting boundaries is to clearly communicate your needs and expectations to others. This can involve being assertive and standing firm in your decisions, even if it may be difficult or uncomfortable. By clearly expressing your boundaries and expectations, you can prevent misunderstandings and ensure that your needs are respected. It is also important to be consistent in enforcing your boundaries and not waver in the face of resistance or pushback from others. Remember that setting boundaries is not about being mean or selfish, but rather about taking care of yourself and ensuring that your needs are met.

Another tip for setting boundaries is to learn to say "no" when necessary. It can be tempting to agree to every request or favor that comes your way, but this can lead to feelings of overwhelm and resentment. By learning to say no when you need to, you can protect your time, energy, and mental health, and ensure that you are able to focus on what is truly important to you. Remember that saying no is not a sign of weakness, but rather a sign of self-respect and self-care.

It is okay to prioritize yourself and your needs, even if it means saying no to others.

It is also important to practice self-compassion when setting boundaries. It can be easy to feel guilty or selfish when setting boundaries, but it is important to remember that taking care of yourself is not a luxury, but a necessity. By practicing self-compassion and acknowledging your own needs and limitations, you can set boundaries that are in alignment with your values and priorities. Remember that setting boundaries is an act of self-love and self-care, and that you deserve to prioritize your own well-being and happiness. By making self-care a priority in your daily routine, you can invest in your own well-being and ensure that you have the energy and resilience to handle life's challenges. Setting boundaries can help you protect your time, energy, and mental health, and ensure that your needs are respected and met. By clearly communicating your boundaries, learning to say no when necessary, and practicing self-compassion, you can create a healthier and more fulfilling life for yourself. Remember that taking care of yourself is not selfish, but necessary for living a happy and balanced life.

- Incorporating meditation into a holistic self-care routine

Incorporating meditation into a holistic self-care routine can be a powerful tool for improving overall well-being and managing stress. Meditation has been practiced for thousands of years and has been shown to have numerous benefits for both the mind and body. By taking time to quiet the mind and focus on the present moment, individuals can reduce anxiety and increase feelings of calm and relaxation. In addition, regular meditation practice has been linked to improved concentration, better sleep, and enhanced emotional well-being.

One of the key benefits of incorporating meditation into a holistic self-care routine is its ability to help individuals manage stress more effectively. In today's fast-paced world, stress is a common problem that can have a negative impact on both physical and mental health. By practicing meditation regularly, individuals can learn to quiet the mind and body and reduce the negative effects of stress. By taking time to sit quietly and focus on the breath, individuals can cultivate a sense of inner peace and calm that can help them cope with the challenges of everyday life.

In addition to stress management, meditation can also have a positive impact on mental health. Research has shown that regular meditation practice can help individuals reduce symptoms of anxiety and depression. By focusing on the present moment and letting go of negative thoughts and emotions, individuals can cultivate a sense of mindfulness and self-awareness that can help them better navigate their emotions and improve their overall well-being. Meditation can also help individuals increase their self-compassion and develop a greater sense of empathy and connection with others.

Furthermore, incorporating meditation into a holistic self-care routine can have numerous benefits for physical health as well. Research has shown that regular meditation practice can help lower blood pressure, improve immune function, and reduce inflammation in the body. By cultivating a sense of relaxation and calm through meditation, individuals can help their bodies heal and repair from the effects of chronic stress and improve their overall health and well-being. In addition, meditation can also help individuals improve their sleep quality and enhance their overall energy levels, allowing them to feel more rested and rejuvenated throughout the day.

Incorporating meditation into a holistic self-care routine does not have to be complicated or time-consuming. Even just a few minutes of meditation each day can have a significant impact on overall well-being. To get started, find a quiet space where you can sit comfortably and without distractions. Close your eyes and take a few deep breaths to center yourself and bring your focus to the present moment. You can choose to focus on your breath, a mantra, or a visualization to help quiet the mind and cultivate a sense of peace and calm.

As you continue to practice meditation regularly, you may begin to notice small shifts in your overall well-being. You may feel more centered and grounded, less reactive to stressors, and more in tune with your emotions and needs. Over time, you may find that your meditation practice becomes a valuable tool for managing stress, improving mental health, and enhancing physical well-being. Remember that incorporating meditation into your self-care routine is a journey, and it is important to be patient with yourself as you explore this powerful practice. With time and practice, you may find that meditation becomes an essential part of your holistic self-care routine, helping you live a happier, healthier, and more balanced life.

Chapter 17: Meditation for Emotional Regulation

- TECHNIQUES FOR MANAGING and regulating emotions through meditation

Emotions play a crucial role in our daily lives, influencing our thoughts, decisions, and behaviors. It is essential to understand how to manage and regulate these emotions to maintain mental well-being and overall emotional stability. One effective technique for achieving this is through meditation. Meditation is a practice that has been used for centuries to cultivate mindfulness, focus, and emotional regulation. By incorporating specific meditation techniques into our daily routine, we can learn to better understand and manage our emotions, leading to improved mental health and a more balanced emotional state.

One of the primary benefits of meditation is its ability to increase self-awareness. By practicing mindfulness meditation, individuals can become more attuned to their thoughts, feelings, and bodily sensations. This heightened self-awareness allows individuals to recognize when they are experiencing strong emotions and to better understand the underlying causes of those emotions. Through regular meditation practice, individuals can learn to observe their emotions without judgment, allowing them to respond to challenging situations with greater awareness and control.

Another key aspect of managing and regulating emotions through meditation is the development of emotional resilience. By practicing meditation regularly, individuals can cultivate a greater sense of inner peace and calm. This sense of inner calm can help individuals navigate difficult emotions with more ease and grace, avoiding becoming overwhelmed or reactive in the face of challenging situations. By developing emotional resilience through meditation, individuals can build a stronger sense of emotional stability, enabling them to more effectively cope with stress and adversity.

In addition to increasing self-awareness and emotional resilience, meditation can also help individuals cultivate a greater sense of compassion and empathy towards themselves and others. By practicing loving-kindness meditation, individuals can cultivate feelings of warmth, kindness, and compassion towards themselves and others. This practice can help individuals develop a more positive and caring relationship with themselves, leading to greater self-acceptance and self-compassion. In turn, this increased sense of self-compassion can help individuals manage and regulate their emotions more effectively, as they learn to treat themselves with greater kindness and understanding.

One of the most powerful techniques for managing and regulating emotions through meditation is the practice of mindfulness. Mindfulness meditation involves bringing one's attention to the present moment, observing thoughts, feelings, and sensations without judgment. By practicing mindfulness meditation, individuals can learn to bring awareness to their emotions as they arise, allowing them to observe and acknowledge those emotions without becoming overwhelmed or reactive. This ability to observe emotions with equanimity can help individuals cultivate a greater sense of emotional regulation, enabling them to respond to challenging situations with greater clarity and composure. By practicing mindfulness, loving-kindness, and other meditation techniques regularly, individuals can cultivate greater self-awareness, emotional resilience, compassion, and mindfulness. These qualities can help individuals develop a more balanced and healthy relationship with their emotions, enabling them to navigate difficult situations with greater ease and grace. Through the practice of meditation, individuals can learn to cultivate a greater sense of emotional regulation, leading to improved mental well-being and overall emotional stability.

- Improving emotional intelligence and resilience with meditation

Emotional intelligence and resilience are two vital components of mental well-being that can greatly impact one's ability to navigate life's challenges and setbacks. While these traits may come more naturally to some individuals, they can also be cultivated and strengthened through various practices, one of which is meditation.

Meditation is a centuries-old practice that involves focusing the mind and increasing awareness of the present moment. Through mindfulness meditation, individuals can learn to recognize and respond to their emotions in a more constructive and balanced way. By developing this level of self-awareness, individuals can enhance their emotional intelligence, or EQ, which is the ability to recognize, understand, and manage one's own emotions and the emotions of others.

Research has shown that engaging in regular meditation practices can lead to significant improvements in emotional intelligence. For example, a study published in the journal Mindfulness found that participants who completed an eight-week mindfulness meditation program showed increases in self-awareness, self-regulation, and empathy, all key components of emotional intelligence. These improvements can lead to better relationships, increased resilience, and a greater sense of well-being.

In addition to enhancing emotional intelligence, meditation can also strengthen resilience, which is the ability to bounce back from setbacks, adapt to change, and cope with stress and adversity. By practicing mindfulness meditation, individuals can develop a greater sense of inner calm, clarity, and perspective, which can help them navigate life's challenges with greater ease and grace.

One of the key ways in which meditation improves resilience is by helping individuals cultivate a more positive outlook on life. Through meditation practices such as loving-kindness meditation, individuals can learn to cultivate feelings of compassion, gratitude, and acceptance, which can help them cope with difficult situations and setbacks. Research has shown that individuals who engage in regular meditation practices report higher levels of resilience and lower levels of stress and anxiety.

Furthermore, meditation can also help individuals develop greater emotional regulation skills, which are essential for building resilience. By learning to observe their emotions without judgment and respond to them in a calm and balanced way, individuals can build the emotional strength and flexibility needed to navigate life's ups and downs with greater ease. This ability to regulate emotions can help individuals maintain a sense of equilibrium and composure even in the face of difficult circumstances. By practicing mindfulness meditation, individuals can enhance their self-awareness, emotional regulation, and empathy, all of which are key components of emotional intelligence. Additionally, meditation can help individuals cultivate a more positive outlook on life, develop greater emotional regulation skills, and build the inner strength and flexibility needed to navigate life's challenges with greater ease and grace. Ultimately, by incorporating meditation into their daily routine, individuals can strengthen their mental well-being and enhance their ability to cope with stress, adversity, and change.

- Cultivating a sense of calm and stability during challenging situations

In today's fast-paced and unpredictable world, it is essential to cultivate a sense of calm and stability during challenging situations. The ability to remain grounded and composed when faced with adversity can have a significant impact on one's overall well-being and success. It is natural to feel overwhelmed or anxious when confronted with difficult circumstances, but by developing strategies to help maintain a sense of calm, individuals can navigate challenges more effectively and with greater resilience.

One of the key components of cultivating a sense of calm and stability during challenging situations is practicing mindfulness. Mindfulness involves being fully present in the moment and acknowledging one's thoughts and feelings without judgment. By cultivating a mindfulness practice, individuals can learn to observe their reactions to difficult situations and respond in a more measured and thoughtful manner. This can help reduce feelings of overwhelm and create a sense of inner peace and clarity.

In addition to mindfulness, developing a strong support system can also be instrumental in maintaining a sense of calm during challenging times. Surrounding oneself with supportive and understanding friends, family members, or colleagues can provide a sense of reassurance and comfort when facing difficult situations. Having a safe and non-judgmental space to share one's thoughts and feelings can help individuals process emotions and gain perspective on the challenges they are facing.

Another important aspect of cultivating calm and stability during challenging situations is practicing self-care. Taking care of one's physical, emotional, and mental well-being is crucial for maintaining a sense of balance and resilience in the face of adversity. This can include engaging in activities that bring joy and relaxation, such as exercise, meditation, or spending time in nature. Prioritizing self-care can help individuals recharge and replenish their energy levels, making it easier to cope with stress and uncertainty.

Furthermore, developing a growth mindset can be a powerful tool in cultivating a sense of calm and stability during challenging situations. A growth mindset involves viewing challenges as opportunities for learning and growth, rather than obstacles to be avoided. By reframing difficult situations in this way, individuals can approach challenges with a sense of curiosity and optimism, rather than fear or resistance. This can help foster resilience and adaptability, allowing individuals to navigate adversity with greater confidence and resourcefulness. By practicing mindfulness, building a strong support system, prioritizing self-care, and developing a growth mindset, individuals can enhance their ability to cope with adversity and approach challenges with greater resilience and grace. By integrating these strategies into one's daily life, individuals can cultivate a sense of inner peace and strength that will serve them well in the face of life's inevitable ups and downs.

Chapter 18: Connecting with Nature through Meditation

- BENEFITS OF NATURE-based meditation for mental health

Nature-based meditation, also known as ecotherapy or outdoor meditation, is a practice that involves meditating in natural settings such as forests, beaches, or mountains. This form of meditation is gaining popularity in recent years due to its numerous benefits for mental health. When combined with meditation, the benefits are even more pronounced, as mindfulness and connection to nature can work together to enhance mental health outcomes.

One of the key benefits of nature-based meditation is its ability to reduce stress and promote relaxation. The sights, sounds, and smells of nature can have a calming effect on our nervous system, helping to lower levels of cortisol, the stress hormone. When we meditate in a natural setting, we are able to focus on our breathing and surroundings, allowing us to let go of worries and distractions and enter a state of deep relaxation. This can be especially beneficial for those who suffer from chronic stress or anxiety, as regular nature-based meditation practice can help to reset the nervous system and promote a sense of calm and well-being.

In addition to reducing stress, nature-based meditation can also help to alleviate symptoms of anxiety and depression. Research has shown that spending time in nature can boost levels of serotonin, the "feel-good" neurotransmitter that plays a key role in regulating mood. By combining meditation with nature, individuals can cultivate a sense of mindfulness and presence that can help to ease symptoms of anxiety and depression. Being in a natural setting can also provide a sense of grounding and connection to something larger than ourselves, which can be comforting and healing for those struggling with mental health challenges.

Nature-based meditation has also been shown to improve cognitive function and focus. When we meditate in nature, our brains are able to rest and recharge, allowing us to come back to our daily lives with a renewed sense of clarity and purpose. Research has shown that spending time in nature can enhance cognitive function, attention, and memory, making it an ideal setting for meditation practice.

Another benefit of nature-based meditation is its ability to foster a sense of connection and interconnectedness. When we meditate in nature, we become more attuned to the rhythms and cycles of the natural world, helping us to feel a sense of belonging and interconnectedness with all living beings. This sense of connection can be deeply healing and restorative, helping us to feel more grounded, centered, and at peace. By bringing mindfulness and meditation into our relationship with nature, we can cultivate a sense of reverence and gratitude for the beauty and wonder of the natural world, leading to a greater sense of fulfillment and well-being. By spending time in nature and combining meditation with mindfulness practices, individuals can reduce stress, anxiety, and depression, improve cognitive function and focus, and foster a sense of connection and interconnectedness. Whether it's taking a mindful walk in the woods, sitting by a babbling brook, or practicing yoga on the beach, there are countless ways to incorporate nature-based meditation into our daily lives. By making time for nature and mindfulness, we can reap the countless benefits for our mental health and well-being, leading to a more balanced, centered, and fulfilling life.

- Techniques for incorporating nature into meditation practice

Meditation has long been practiced as a way to cultivate mindfulness, reduce stress, and improve overall well-being. Incorporating nature into meditation practice can enhance these benefits by connecting us to the natural world and fostering a sense of peace and tranquility. There are a variety of techniques that can be used to bring nature into our meditation practice, from practicing outdoors to using nature-inspired imagery and sounds. By incorporating nature into our meditation practice, we can deepen our connection to the world around us and enhance the benefits of our meditation practice.

One of the simplest ways to incorporate nature into our meditation practice is to practice outdoors. Spending time in nature has been shown to have numerous benefits for our mental and physical well-being, such as reducing stress, improving mood, and increasing feelings of connectedness. By practicing meditation outdoors, we can enhance these benefits by immersing ourselves in the sights, sounds, and sensations of the natural world. Find a quiet spot in a park, forest, or garden where you can sit comfortably without distractions. Close your eyes and take a few deep breaths, feeling the earth beneath you and the sun or breeze on your skin. As you meditate, allow yourself to be present with the sounds of birds singing, leaves rustling, or water flowing. Let the beauty and tranquility of nature wash over you, grounding you in the present moment and deepening your connection to the natural world.

Another technique for incorporating nature into meditation practice is to use nature-inspired imagery and sounds. Close your eyes and imagine yourself in a peaceful natural setting, such as a tranquil forest, a serene beach, or a majestic mountain. Visualize the colors, textures, and scents of this setting, allowing yourself to feel as if you are truly there. You can also listen to recordings of nature sounds, such as birdsong, ocean waves, or rainfall, to create a calming and immersive meditation experience. As you meditate, focus on these images and sounds, allowing them to bring a sense of peace and serenity to your practice. By immersing yourself in nature-inspired imagery and sounds, you can enhance your meditation practice and cultivate a deeper connection to the natural world.

Incorporating nature into meditation practice can also be done through mindful nature walks. Take a leisurely stroll through a park, garden, or nature reserve, paying close attention to the sights, sounds, and sensations around you. Notice the colors of the flowers, the shapes of the trees, and the textures of the earth beneath your feet. Listen to the songs of the birds, the rustling of the leaves, and the flow of the water. Feel the warmth of the sun on your skin, the coolness of the breeze, and the solidity of the ground beneath you. As you walk, allow yourself to be fully present in the moment, taking in the beauty and wonder of the natural world. Use this mindful nature walk as a form of walking meditation, focusing on your breath and the sensations of each step, allowing nature to be your guide and teacher.

Practicing yoga in nature is another powerful way to incorporate nature into meditation practice. Yoga is a mind-body practice that combines physical postures, breath work, and meditation to cultivate mindfulness and promote holistic well-being. Practicing yoga outdoors allows us to connect with the elements of nature – the earth, water, fire, air, and ether – and align our energy with the natural rhythms of the world. Find a quiet spot outdoors where you can lay down a yoga mat or blanket and practice your asanas under the open sky. As you move through your yoga sequence, focus on your breath and the sensations in your body, allowing yourself to be fully present in the moment. Feel the earth supporting you in each pose, the wind caressing your skin, and the sun energizing your spirit. By practicing yoga in nature, you can deepen your connection to the natural world, strengthen your mind-body-spirit connection, and enhance the benefits of your meditation practice. From practicing outdoors to using nature-inspired imagery and sounds, mindful nature walks to practicing yoga in nature, there are a variety of ways to bring the beauty and tranquility of nature into our meditation practice. By immersing ourselves in the sights, sounds, and sensations of the natural world, we can cultivate mindfulness, reduce stress, and improve our overall well-being. So next time you meditate, consider incorporating nature into your practice and let the wonders of the natural world guide you on your journey to inner peace and tranquility.

- Finding peace and tranquility in the natural world through mindfulness

Finding peace and tranquility in the natural world through mindfulness is a powerful practice that has been utilized for centuries by individuals seeking to connect with themselves and their surroundings on a deeper level. Mindfulness, a form of meditation that involves being fully present and aware of the present moment, can be greatly enhanced by immersing oneself in the beauty and serenity of nature. This connection with the natural world allows individuals to let go of mental chatter, stress, and worries, and instead focus on the sights, sounds, and sensations that surround them.

Mindfulness in nature is about slowing down and truly experiencing the world around us. It involves using all of our senses to take in the beauty and wonder of our surroundings, from the vibrant colors of the flowers to the gentle rustling of the leaves in the wind. When we are fully present and engaged with nature, we can feel a sense of calm and peace wash over us, helping to alleviate the stresses and anxieties of everyday life. This practice can also help to increase our appreciation for the natural world and the interconnectedness of all living beings.

One of the key benefits of practicing mindfulness in nature is the opportunity to cultivate a sense of gratitude and awe for the world around us. When we take the time to pause and truly observe the beauty of a sunrise or the majesty of a towering tree, we can't help but feel a sense of wonder and appreciation for the natural world. This sense of gratitude can help to shift our perspective and bring more positivity and joy into our lives. By focusing on the present moment and letting go of our worries and concerns, we can experience a deep sense of peace and tranquility that can be difficult to find in our fast-paced, technology-driven world.

Another benefit of practicing mindfulness in nature is the opportunity to connect with our inner selves and foster a sense of self-awareness and introspection. When we immerse ourselves in the natural world and let go of distractions, we create space to explore our thoughts, emotions, and innermost desires. This introspection can help us gain clarity and insight into our lives, allowing us to better understand ourselves and our place in the world. By being present in the moment and observing our thoughts and feelings without judgment, we can learn to cultivate a healthier relationship with ourselves and cultivate a greater sense of inner peace and tranquility.

In addition to the mental and emotional benefits of mindfulness in nature, there are also physical benefits to be gained from spending time in the natural world. Being in nature has been shown to reduce stress levels, lower blood pressure, and boost overall well-being. The fresh air, natural light, and peaceful surroundings can have a calming and rejuvenating effect on the body, helping to restore balance and harmony to our physical selves. By practicing mindfulness in nature, we can reduce the negative effects of chronic stress and improve our overall health and well-being.

Mindfulness in nature is a practice that is accessible to everyone, regardless of age, background, or experience level. Whether you live in a bustling city or a rural area, there are always opportunities to connect with the natural world and experience moments of peace and tranquility. Simply taking a walk in a nearby park, sitting by a lake, or spending time in your backyard can provide the perfect setting for practicing mindfulness in nature. By being fully present and engaged with our surroundings, we can cultivate a greater sense of peace, calm, and well-being in our lives. By immersing ourselves in the beauty and serenity of nature, we can let go of our worries and stresses, cultivate a sense of gratitude and awe, and connect with our inner selves in a meaningful way. The practice of mindfulness in nature offers a myriad of benefits for our mental, emotional, and physical well-being, and can help us lead more fulfilling and balanced lives. So, take some time to step outside, breathe in the fresh air, and embrace the beauty of the natural world – you may just find the peace and tranquility you've been searching for.

Chapter 19: Reflection and Integration

- IMPORTANCE OF REFLECTING on the meditation journey

Reflecting on the meditation journey is a crucial aspect of one's practice that allows for growth, insight, and transformation. It is through self-reflection that individuals are able to deepen their understanding of their thoughts, emotions, and behaviors, and cultivate a greater sense of self-awareness and mindfulness. By taking the time to reflect on our meditation experiences, we are able to gain valuable insights into our inner workings and develop a deeper connection with ourselves.

One of the key benefits of reflecting on the meditation journey is the ability to identify patterns and habits that may be holding us back or causing us distress. By being mindful of these patterns, we are better equipped to address them and make positive changes in our lives.

Moreover, reflecting on the meditation journey allows us to cultivate a sense of gratitude and appreciation for the present moment. As we look back on our past experiences and growth, we are able to acknowledge the progress we have made and celebrate our achievements, no matter how small they may seem. This sense of gratitude can help us to stay motivated and inspired on our meditation journey, and remind us of the importance of being present and living in the moment.

In addition, reflecting on the meditation journey can help us to develop a greater sense of compassion and empathy for ourselves and others. By taking the time to reflect on our own struggles, challenges, and triumphs, we are able to cultivate a deeper sense of understanding and acceptance of ourselves. This self-compassion can then extend to others, as we become more empathetic and compassionate towards the struggles and challenges that they may be facing.

Furthermore, reflecting on the meditation journey can help to deepen our spiritual practice and connection to the larger world around us. By being mindful of our thoughts, emotions, and behaviors, we are able to tap into a deeper sense of inner peace and wisdom that can guide us on our path towards personal growth and enlightenment. Through reflection, we are able to connect more deeply with our true selves and gain a better understanding of our place in the world. By taking the time to reflect on our experiences, we are able to gain valuable insights into our inner workings, identify patterns and habits that may be holding us back, cultivate a greater sense of self-awareness and mindfulness, develop a sense of gratitude and appreciation for the present moment, and deepen our spiritual practice and connection to the larger world around us. Through reflection, we are able to tap into a deeper sense of inner peace and wisdom that can guide us on our path towards personal growth and enlightenment.

- Strategies for integrating mindfulness practices into daily life

Mindfulness is a powerful practice that has gained popularity in recent years for its ability to reduce stress, increase focus and productivity, and improve overall mental well-being. Integrating mindfulness practices into daily life can have a profound impact on our health and happiness. In this article, we will explore strategies for incorporating mindfulness into our daily routines in a practical and sustainable way.

One of the most effective ways to integrate mindfulness into daily life is to establish a daily meditation practice. Meditation is a core component of mindfulness and can help us cultivate awareness and presence in our daily activities. Set aside a few minutes each day to sit quietly and focus on your breath. This can help calm the mind, reduce stress, and improve concentration. Start with just a few minutes each day and gradually increase the duration as you become more comfortable with the practice.

Another strategy for integrating mindfulness into daily life is to practice mindfulness throughout the day. This can be done by bringing awareness to everyday activities such as eating, walking, or even washing the dishes. Pay attention to the sensations, thoughts, and emotions that arise during these activities without judgment. This can help us stay present and engaged in the moment, rather than being swept away by distractions or worries.

In addition to formal meditation practices and mindfulness in daily activities, another important strategy for integrating mindfulness into daily life is to cultivate a mindset of mindfulness. This involves being consciously aware of your thoughts, emotions, and actions throughout the day. Notice when your mind starts to wander or when you feel stressed or anxious. Instead of getting caught up in these negative patterns, gently guide your attention back to the present moment and take a few deep breaths. This can help break the cycle of rumination and bring a sense of calm and clarity to your day.

Furthermore, incorporating mindfulness into daily life can also involve setting intentions and goals that align with your values and priorities. Take some time to reflect on what is important to you and what you want to cultivate in your life. This can help provide a sense of direction and purpose, which can enhance your overall well-being. By aligning your actions with your values, you can create a sense of coherence and harmony in your life, leading to greater fulfillment and satisfaction.

Moreover, integrating mindfulness into daily life can also involve connecting with others in a mindful way. Practice active listening and being fully present with those around you. This can help deepen your relationships and foster a sense of connection and understanding. By being present and attentive in your interactions with others, you can cultivate empathy, compassion, and kindness, which can enhance your overall well-being and happiness. By incorporating strategies such as daily meditation, mindfulness in everyday activities, cultivating a mindset of mindfulness, setting intentions and goals, and connecting with others in a mindful way, we can cultivate greater awareness, presence, and fulfillment in our daily lives. Through consistent practice and dedication, we can experience the benefits of mindfulness and lead a more balanced and harmonious life.

- Setting intentions for continued growth and inner calm

As we navigate the complexities of our daily lives, it can be easy to get caught up in the hustle and bustle of our responsibilities and commitments.

However, in order to truly thrive and find inner peace, it is essential to set intentions for continued growth and inner calm. Setting intentions involves creating a clear vision of what we want to achieve and how we want to feel, and then actively working towards manifesting those desires in our lives.

One key aspect of setting intentions for continued growth and inner calm is the practice of mindfulness. Mindfulness is the practice of bringing one's attention to the present moment, without judgment or attachment. By cultivating mindfulness in our daily lives, we can become more attuned to our thoughts, feelings, and actions, allowing us to make more intentional choices that align with our values and goals. Mindfulness can also help us to cultivate a sense of inner calm and peace, by reducing stress and anxiety and increasing our capacity for self-awareness and self-compassion.

In addition to practicing mindfulness, setting intentions for continued growth and inner calm can also involve setting specific goals and action steps to help us achieve our desired outcomes. This might involve setting goals related to personal or professional development, such as learning a new skill or pursuing a promotion at work. By setting clear, actionable goals and breaking them down into manageable steps, we can create a roadmap for our growth and development and ensure that we are moving in the direction of our intentions.

Another important aspect of setting intentions for continued growth and inner calm is cultivating a positive mindset and self-talk. Our thoughts and beliefs have a powerful impact on our emotions and behaviors, so by adopting a positive and growth-oriented mindset, we can create a more supportive inner dialogue that helps us stay motivated and focused on our intentions. This might involve reframing negative beliefs or limiting beliefs, practicing self-affirmations, or seeking out positive influences and role models who can help us stay inspired and motivated.

Furthermore, setting intentions for continued growth and inner calm also involves prioritizing self-care and self-compassion. In our fast-paced and often demanding world, it can be easy to neglect our own needs and well-being in favor of the needs of others or our external obligations. However, true growth and inner calm require that we take care of ourselves first, so that we can show up as our best selves in our relationships and endeavors. This might involve practicing self-care rituals such as meditation, exercise, or journaling, setting boundaries with others to protect our time and energy, or seeking support from a therapist or coach to help us navigate our inner landscape. By cultivating mindfulness, setting goals, adopting a positive mindset, and prioritizing self-care, we can align our actions with our values and goals, and create a sense of inner peace and harmony that sustains us through life's challenges and opportunities. By approaching this process with intention and dedication, we can cultivate a deeper sense of self-awareness, self-compassion, and resilience, and create a life that is aligned with our deepest desires and aspirations.

Chapter 20: Conclusion

- SUMMARY OF KEY TAKEAWAYS from the book

"The book delves into the importance of emotional intelligence in leadership and how it can significantly impact a leader's effectiveness. The author emphasizes the need for leaders to be self-aware, able to regulate their emotions, display empathy, and adept at managing relationships. By honing these skills, leaders can create a positive work environment, foster collaboration, and inspire their teams to perform at their best. The book also highlights the correlation between emotional intelligence and job performance, showing that leaders with high emotional intelligence tend to be more successful in their roles. "

"Another key takeaway from the book is the importance of fostering a culture of trust within an organization. The author explains how trust is essential for building strong relationships, enhancing communication, and driving productivity. Leaders who prioritize trust create an environment where employees feel safe to speak up, take risks, and innovate. The book also offers strategies for building trust, such as leading by example, being transparent, and honoring commitments. Ultimately, the book underscores how trust is a foundational element of effective leadership and provides actionable steps for leaders to enhance trust within their teams. "

"Furthermore, the book emphasizes the significance of adaptability in leadership. In today's fast-paced and ever-changing business environment, leaders must be flexible and open to change in order to navigate uncertainty and drive success. The author discusses the importance of being able to pivot quickly, make decisions in ambiguous situations, and learn from failures.

Leaders who embrace adaptability are better equipped to lead their teams through transitions, disruptions, and challenges. The book also highlights the value of continuous learning and growth mindset in fostering adaptability. By continuously developing new skills and knowledge, leaders can stay relevant and agile in the face of change. "

"Lastly, the book emphasizes the significance of diversity and inclusion in leadership. The author discusses how a diverse team can bring a wide range of perspectives, ideas, and experiences to the table, leading to more innovative solutions and better decision-making. Inclusive leadership involves creating a culture where every team member feels valued, respected, and supported. Leaders who prioritize diversity and inclusion are more likely to attract top talent, improve employee morale, and drive business performance. The book also explores the benefits of diversity training, mentorship programs, and inclusive policies in fostering a diverse and inclusive workplace. Ultimately, the book underscores the value of diversity and inclusion in leadership and provides practical strategies for creating a more inclusive organizational culture. "

- Encouragement for continued meditation practice and self-care

Meditation is a powerful practice that has been used for centuries to promote relaxation, mindfulness, and overall well-being. It involves focusing the mind and eliminating distractions in order to achieve a state of calm and inner peace. While meditation can be challenging at times, especially for beginners, the benefits are well worth the effort. By taking the time to quiet the mind and connect with the present moment, individuals can reduce stress, improve concentration, and cultivate a sense of inner harmony.

One of the key reasons to continue a meditation practice is the positive impact it can have on mental health. Research has shown that regular meditation can help reduce symptoms of anxiety, depression, and other mental health conditions. By incorporating meditation into your daily routine, you can learn to better manage your emotions and develop a greater sense of self-awareness. This can lead to improved relationships, increased productivity, and a greater sense of overall well-being.

In addition to its mental health benefits, meditation can also have a positive impact on physical health. Studies have shown that regular meditation can help reduce blood pressure, improve immune function, and even slow the aging process. By taking care of your mind through meditation, you are also taking care of your body. This mind-body connection is a powerful tool for promoting overall health and wellness.

It is important to remember that meditation is a skill that takes time and practice to develop. Like any skill, the more you practice, the better you will become. If you are struggling with your meditation practice, it is important to be patient with yourself and not give up. Remember that everyone has their own unique way of meditating, and what works for one person may not work for another. Experiment with different techniques, such as mindfulness meditation, loving-kindness meditation, or body scan meditation, to find what resonates with you.

Another important aspect of continued meditation practice is self-care. In today's fast-paced world, it is easy to neglect our own well-being in favor of work, family, and other responsibilities. However, taking the time to care for yourself is essential for maintaining a healthy and balanced life. Meditation can be a powerful tool for self-care, as it allows you to take a break from the chaos of daily life and tune in to your own needs and desires. By making time for meditation each day, you are sending a clear message to yourself that you are worth taking care of. By continuing your meditation practice and making self-care a priority, you can cultivate a greater sense of well-being and inner peace. Remember to be patient with yourself, explore different meditation techniques, and make time for self-care each day. With dedication and commitment, you can reap the many benefits of meditation and live a more balanced and fulfilling life.

- Final thoughts on finding inner calm through essential meditations

Meditation has long been recognized as a powerful tool for finding inner calm and cultivating a sense of peace and tranquility within oneself. Through the practice of various meditation techniques, individuals can tap into their inner resources and develop a greater sense of self-awareness and mindfulness. Essential in this process is the ability to focus the mind and let go of distractions, allowing for a deepening of one's connection to the present moment and a heightened awareness of one's thoughts and emotions. By engaging in regular meditation practice, individuals can gain greater insight into their inner landscape, learning to navigate the complexities of their minds with greater ease and clarity.

One of the key benefits of meditation is its ability to cultivate a sense of inner calm and relaxation. Through regular practice, individuals can train their minds to become less reactive to external stimuli and more at peace with their inner thoughts and feelings. By learning to observe their thoughts without judgment, individuals can develop a greater sense of emotional resilience and a deeper capacity for self-reflection. This can lead to a greater sense of inner peace and contentment, as individuals learn to let go of the stresses and worries that can often cloud their minds.

Another important aspect of finding inner calm through meditation is the cultivation of mindfulness. Mindfulness is the practice of paying attention to the present moment with openness and curiosity, without judgment or attachment. By developing a mindfulness practice, individuals can become more attuned to their thoughts, emotions, and physical sensations, helping them to gain a greater sense of self-awareness and self-acceptance. This can lead to a greater sense of inner peace and contentment, as individuals learn to let go of the past and future and fully engage with the present moment.

In addition to cultivating inner calm and mindfulness, meditation can also help individuals develop a greater sense of compassion and empathy towards themselves and others. Through the practice of loving-kindness meditation, individuals can cultivate feelings of goodwill, kindness, and compassion towards themselves and others. This can lead to a greater sense of connection and empathy with others, as individuals learn to let go of judgment and criticism and embrace a more compassionate and loving attitude towards themselves and those around them. This can lead to a greater sense of inner peace and contentment, as individuals learn to let go of anger, resentment, and negativity and cultivate a more positive and loving mindset. By cultivating a regular meditation practice, individuals can tap into their inner resources and develop a greater sense of self-awareness, mindfulness, and compassion. This can lead to a greater sense of inner peace and contentment, as individuals learn to let go of stress, worry, and negativity and embrace a more positive and loving mindset. Through the practice of essential meditations, individuals can find a deep sense of calm and tranquility within themselves, paving the way for greater happiness and fulfillment in their lives.